GOLDEN
EAGLE
COUNTRY

ALFRED A. KNOPF

NEW YORK

1975

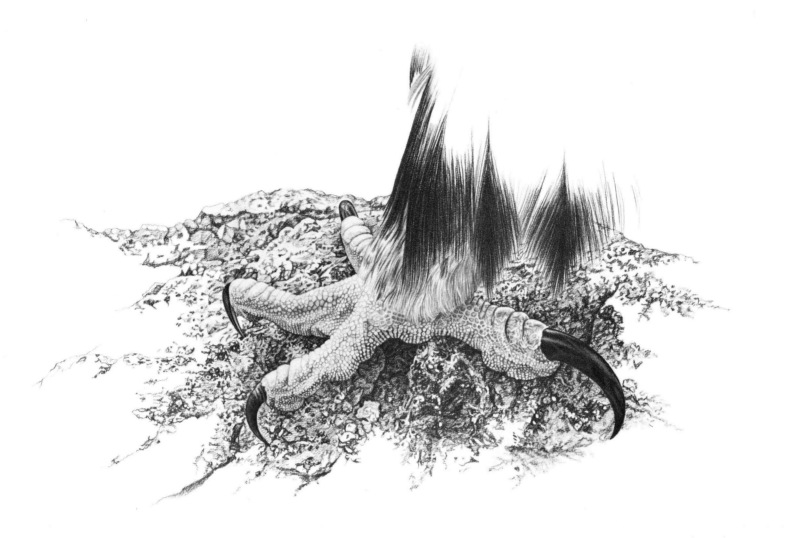

GOLDEN EAGLE COUNTRY

by Richard R. Olendorff

Drawings by Robert Katona

THIS IS A BORZOI BOOK
PUBLISHED BY ALFRED A. KNOPF, INC.

Library of Congress Cataloging in Publication Data

Olendorff, Richard   Golden eagle country.
Bibliography: p.
1. Birds of prey.   2. Golden eagle.   I. Title.
QL696.F3038   598.9′1   75-8211
ISBN 0-394-48292-1

Manufactured in the United States of America
First Edition

To Sherri, my wife and my reason.

CONTENTS

Foreword by Dean Amadon   xi

Acknowledgments   xiii

Author's Note   xv

1 Nature's Golden Touch   *5*

2 His Needs Are His Message   *17*

3 A Long and Interesting History   *29*

4 Why Raptors?   *41*

5 A Year Later   *51*

6 "You Think and I'll Drive!"   *65*

7 Setting a Summer Stage   *77*

8 In One Misplaced Second   *89*

9 Three Ounces of Smallish Might   *101*

10 In Search of New Arrivals   *111*

11 Naïve Hopes   *125*

12 Natural Problems   *139*

13 A Solid Experience   *151*

14 "Ever Stop for Tea?"   *169*

15 Fledging: A Hollow Promise   *183*

Epilogue   *197*

ILLUSTRATIONS

A Map of Golden Eagle Country   *by Anita Karl*   3

Winter Windmill with Eagle   9

Adult Golden Eagles   12

Cottontail Rabbit   15

Horned Lark   19

Bald Eagle   24

Badgers in Dispute   32

Young Coyote Atop a Cliff   35

Oil Well Eyrie   46

Immature Red-Tailed Hawk   53

Mallards   54

Meadowlark   59

Immature Red-tailed Hawk in Flight   67

Prairie Falcons in Courtship   73

Burrowing Owl   78

Great Horned Owl and Nest   85

Observation Blind   91

Golden Eagle Nest   95

Golden Eagle Foot   97

American Avocet Feeding   102

Mountain Plover   109

Mourning Dove   115

Soaring Swainson's Hawks   119

Dark Phase Ferruginous Hawk   121

Cliff Swallows   129

Long-billed Curlew   135

Peregrine Falcon   136

Yucca Plant   138

Female Lark Bunting   141

Three-week-old Eaglet   142

Short-horned Lizard   146

Prairie Rattlesnake   153

Bull Snake   163

Adult Female Golden Eagle Feeding Her Young   171

Ferruginous Hawk Nest with Two Young   177

Three Prairie Falcons Ready to Fledge   182

Young Golden Eagles in Nest   187

Young Ferruginous Hawk on Post   191

Young Eagles Ready to Fledge   195

Head of Immature Golden Eagle   201

FOREWORD

by Dean Amadon

The golden eagle is a rare bird in eastern North America, although a few are seen each autumn at Hawk Mountain, Pennsylvania, and other flyways, and an occasional pair still nests in the more remote mountains of New England. Our "king of birds" is much more common in the West, yet it remains less known to the general public than its conspicuously marked relative, the bald eagle. This is unfortunate, as the golden eagle is in most respects a finer bird—surer on the wing, more dashing in pursuit of prey, and less inclined to take carrion. Indeed it is the same eagle that was the symbol of the legions of Caesar and Napoleon.

Richard R. Olendorff is especially well qualified to write of the golden eagle—not only as a beautiful and spectacular bird of prey but as an important member of the ecosystem of our continent. His boyhood in Alaska was followed by years of biological training in several habitats of golden eagles and other raptorial birds in the lower forty-eight states, as well as time spent probing the growth and physiology of such birds in the laboratory. He was equally diligent in gleaning information from the literature, old and recent; indeed, he and his wife, Sharon, had earlier compiled and published in three parts a bibliography listing thousands of papers and books on eagles, falcons, hawks, and other birds of prey. Meanwhile, he had also found time, while still a student to edit several volumes of newsletters and the journals of two professional organizations. This was followed by a post-doctoral fellowship under the Chapman Memorial Fund at the American Museum of Natural History in New York, and a field associateship with the Museum spent mostly on the shortgrass prairie and, later, in Bremerton, Washington, where this volume was written.

A complete change of locale has now taken this energetic young man to Washington, D.C., where he and others are organizing a more active interest in wildlife and endangered species for the U.S. Department of the Interior's Bureau of Land Management, which administers thousands of square miles of federal lands in our western states.

Golden Eagle Country acquaints us with the eagle and with its habitat—lonely mesas, prairies, and mountains—by focusing on a few pairs of eagles as they build their eyries, hatch and rear their young. The approach is personal and intimate, the philosophy sound and long range. The settlers who pushed into the semi-arid grasslands a century ago strove heroically, but now all that remains is often a crumbled homestead and a gnarled tree or two—nest sites for eagle or magpie. What will the future bring? Strip mining? A new wave of settlement to push back the eagles and shyer forms of wildlife? No one knows, but Olendorff is not a pessimist. He is convinced that in the long run what is good for eagles, antelope, and, yes, even, perhaps, coyotes, will be good for a jaded mankind, that, in too many places, is being compressed into overly urbanized centers. I hope that he is correct, and that the golden eagle will become a symbol—no longer of martial prowess, but of a harmonious blending of the welfare of man with that of the other creatures sharing our threatened planet.

DEAN AMADON
Department of Ornithology
The American Museum of Natural History
New York
1975

ACKNOWLEDGMENTS

For my ability to gather the information and skills to write this book, I am much indebted to Dr. Dean Amadon, of the American Museum of Natural History. He presented the initial opportunity to conduct the necessary field investigations and also sent me to Angus Cameron, my editor, whose patient advice has been impeccable and farsighted. My major professor at Colorado State University, Dr. Charles G. Wilber, and my undergraduate adviser at the University of Washington, Dr. Frank Richardson, were instrumental in taking me far enough to qualify for postdoctoral studies. Carrying me beyond the goals I set for myself as an ornithologist and as an author is a gift from four superb educators that I will cherish for life.

Funding for my studies has come from the Frank M. Chapman Fund, of the American Museum of Natural History; the National Science Foundation through the International Biological Program Grassland Biome Project; and the Colorado Division of Wildlife.

My grandmother Sallie J. Shaffer was a constant help with the mechanics of writing and in proofreading the numerous revisions. Helpful suggestions have also come from Stephan B. Layman, Frances Hamerstrom, Vern Seifert, Stanley A. Marcus, Kenneth C. Baldwin, and Marjorie Betts. My mother-in-law, Ruth A. Setzer, has borne much of the burden of household responsibilities while my wife, Sherri, has worked both at home and away.

John W. Stoddart, Jr., has been especially competent as a field assistant and technical consultant. Our frequent and lengthy polemic discussions have added considerable depth to our practical knowledge. The viewpoint of Giles Greenfield has also enlarged my perspective.

It is my further good fortune to have Robert Katona as illustrator. Like other artists who have trained or handled many birds of prey, such as George Edward Lodge, Louis Agassiz Fuertes, and David Reid-Henry, Bob Katona can depict not only the beauty but also the personality of eagles, falcons, and hawks. Bob and I are both grateful to the production staff at Alfred A. Knopf, Inc., for their artful preparation of this book for printing.

RICHARD R. OLENDORFF

Department of Ornithology
The American Museum of Natural History
New York
1975

AUTHOR'S NOTE

This is an optimistic book. Some will say it is overly so, and they will continue spreading the false, alarmist notion that all birds of prey are proceeding rapidly toward extinction. Such has not been my experience!

I have found in my studies, for example, that birds of prey are exploiting the potential of living in concert with men. Given half a chance, they will even breed in spite of us. If this were not true, my observations—set in type on the following pages—would not show that nearly a third of all large raptorial birds nesting on two thousand square miles of shortgrass prairie used man-created nest sites. Birds of prey can live close to man: near busy highways, in areas used heavily for recreational purposes, and within a stone's throw of buildings, windmills, and other man-made structures. Some even nest *on* objects like utility poles, windmills, abandoned buildings, and steel towers.

I have also found that nature is still doing many things correctly and on cue. Therefore I do not dwell in this book on issues such as habitat destruction, environmental contamination, poisoning, shooting, electrocution, and the greatly increased activity of many segments of our society. I fully recognize each of these problems, but I believe that most environmental questions relating to predatory birds are answerable through positive educational, scientific, and wildlife programs—as opposed to alarm and panic.

In this book, the reader will learn that the eagle's needs are his message to mankind—and that it is not too late for the eagle or for man! If we will just recognize the potential for coexistence—indeed, the necessary communion—between winged predators and ourselves, then this book will have served its purpose: increasing the possibility that man will give *himself*, as well as eagles and their kin, time to learn to exist side by side.

In recent years, a step in the right direction has been taken, in that all birds of prey have been protected by virtually every state, provincial, and federal government in North America. No one may molest predatory birds in any way, including casual inspection of nests, without written permission from governmental agencies. Thus, although I write about specific places, birds, and observations, I have chosen a fictitious setting—the Eagle Breaks—to further shield the birds whose stories are told herein. Nevertheless, the biological, historical, paleontological, and geological relationships discussed are factual.

R. R. O.

GOLDEN EAGLE COUNTRY

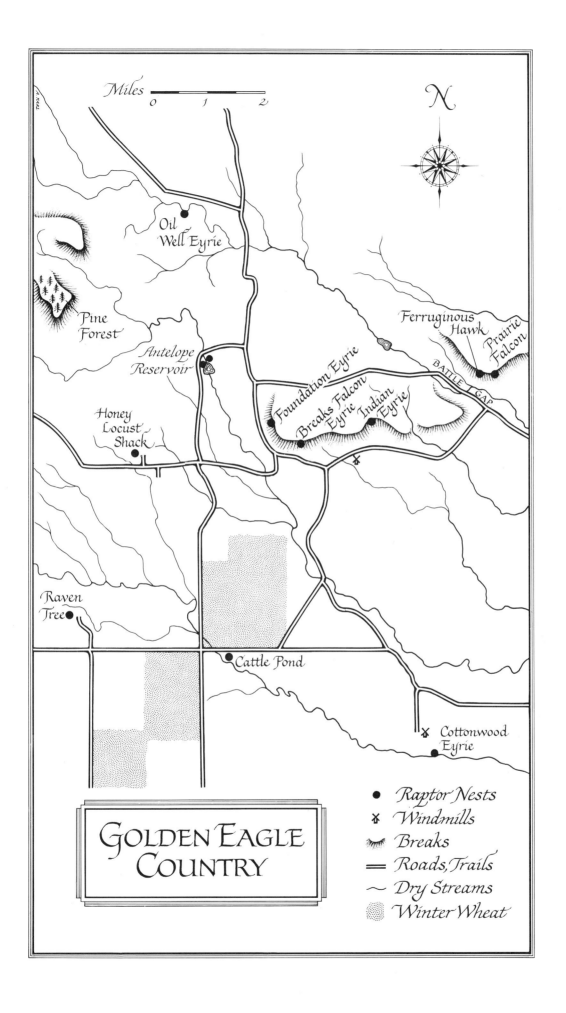

Miles
0   1   2

N

Oil
Well Eyrie

Pine
Forest

Ferruginous
Hawk

Prairie
Falcon

Antelope
Reservoir

Foundation Eyrie

Breaks Falcon
Eyrie

Indian
Eyrie

BATTLE GAP

Honey
Locust
Shack

Raven
Tree

Cattle Pond

Cottonwood
Eyrie

● Raptor Nests
⚐ Windmills
︶ Breaks
═ Roads, Trails
∼ Dry Streams
░ Winter Wheat

GOLDEN EAGLE
COUNTRY

I

NATURE'S GOLDEN TOUCH

Soft powder snow crunched with the sound of grinding teeth as it compacted under the slowly turning tires of my old Volkswagen bus. Nearly seventy thousand miles we had shared, following at every opportunity a way of life many dream about but never attain. The decrepit old roadblock and I had trailed after birds in many parts of the West. We had had our share of good days. Or had we?

Snow makes that squeaking, grinding noise only when it is very cold. Two inches of driven flakes had fallen during the December night, before the temperature dipped from fifteen above to fifteen below zero. It was too cold for more snow but windy enough to build foot-deep drifts in every lee. The wind chill made each venture from my poor-man's limousine a bitter task even in the bright sunlight that poured from a cloudless blue sky onto every drift.

The frigid weather reminded me of my childhood in Alaska, yet I was thousands of miles southeast of Anchorage, on the shortgrass prairie of the western Great Plains. With me was Jack Stoddart, who, though he was one year my junior in age, was ten years my senior in watching grassland birds of prey. When, as a teen-ager, Jack was searching for prairie falcons, golden eagles, and all manner of hawks and owls on the plains, I was chasing peregrine falcons, other golden eagles, and many northern species—gyrfalcons, rough-legged hawks, hawk owls, and snowy owls—in the boreal forest and on the tundra.

I much regret, however, that fewer raptorial birds filled my youth than filled Jack's. Their nests eluded me in the forests and high mountains of my homeland; and I was unable to take part in many of the exciting trips that my Alaskan buddies took in search of raptors—as birds of prey are called collectively. I have strong recollections of George, Dave, and Bill, whom I palled around with in those days, returning from Goodnews Bay, near the Bering Sea, having suffered for a month eating powdered soup and maggot-filled dried salmon stolen from the natives. They had not anticipated the dire effects on one's innards of the sudden change to a nearly liquid diet, or that one has to get dirty enough to stink to keep mosquitoes away. But the bird stories were wild, like running down an adult golden eagle so gorged with young gulls that it could not take off. Their trip to Mount McKinley National Park in a rented Volkswagen bug—the speedometer cable pulled, of course—was a greater success, although there were still stories of labors in vain, such as walking three miles to a gyrfalcon eyrie thought to be only a mile away.

Since I, too, would have cherished the good times—and even the fizzles and failures—the tales of their adventures dispirited me. For I missed the best moments of outdoor life because of self-imposed responsibilities: a paper route, a part-time job at a roller-skating rink, and, later, cleaning train coaches to get money for college.

But life's priorities are ever changing. In retrospect, what I missed as a kid only makes more poignant now the many beautiful experiences I did have on Potter Marsh, near Anchorage, lying in a duckblind watching several hundred whistling swans fly twenty feet over my head to a nearby pond; at Creamer's Dairy, near Fairbanks, where the spring migration of waterfowl rivals the famous fall migration stops on any North American flyway; and in the forests behind Girdwood, where a now famous ski resort scars the beautiful mountains and has probably caused the displacement of most of the local goshawks and great horned owls.

Creamer's Dairy was unusually spectacular during one of my spring visits. Thousands of ducks, geese, and other water birds had come to the small muddy ponds in the rolling pastures to rest and feed before the final day's flight to their breeding grounds north of the Brooks Range. I saw peregrine falcons on fifty different occasions in early May, 1962, during three mornings of sloshing in the fields. Goshawks and red-tailed hawks also plied the wing-filled sky. I had hit the spring migration perfectly!

On the prairie just east of the Rocky Mountains that cold morning—many miles and years away from Creamer's Dairy—Jack and I did not expect to find peregrine falcons; several golden eagles were the likely pleasure of the day, along with a prairie falcon or two, a few ferruginous hawks, and many rough-legged hawks forced south for the winter out of their alluring north country.

Our search for grassland raptors quickly led us to an adult golden eagle sitting on a windmill platform several hundred feet from the road. The wooden tower held the metal sails about twenty feet above the prairie, but a triangularly shaped vane was locked in the same plane as the blades to swivel them constantly sidewise into the wind. The mill had been shut off. No water was needed for cattle, as they had been trucked from the open ranges ahead of winter snows.

The rancher's windmill was a quiet, convenient perch for an eagle in a land where high lookouts were scarce; there were no others in sight. Eagles "want" so badly to be above the ground, where visibility is greater, that they will sit—and even nest!—on whirling windmills. Ranchers discourage nesting on windmills because large eagle nests eventually foul the mill's workings; yet while the cattlemen are on their monotonous patrols of the land, most of them I have met enjoy being greeted by eagles perched atop their equipment. Ranchers can often point out the one windmill on their sprawling pastures that has been adopted by a wintering eagle. And cattlemen do not keep track of eagles to return later to shoot them. If I were an eagle, I would choose to perch near any hundred cattlemen before chancing to sit near one city crackpot. I cannot say the same about some sheepmen, however.

While we watched the perched eagle, the loose trailing feathers of its flanks tossed in the wind. My memory kept flashing back to long winters in Alaska when goshawks were the only common raptorial birds, and two bird watchers were considered a good turnout of the local bird club on a cold day. Most birds of prey had gone south: arctic peregrines were in Central and South America; and most Alaskan golden eagles were probably somewhere in the lower forty-eight states—perhaps sitting on windmill platforms on the shortgrass prairie, soaking up the bright sun on a frosty morning.

"You know, Jake—"

I always called Jack that, in fun, thinking it more rustic but also somewhat belittling, like Rancher Rick or Farmer John.

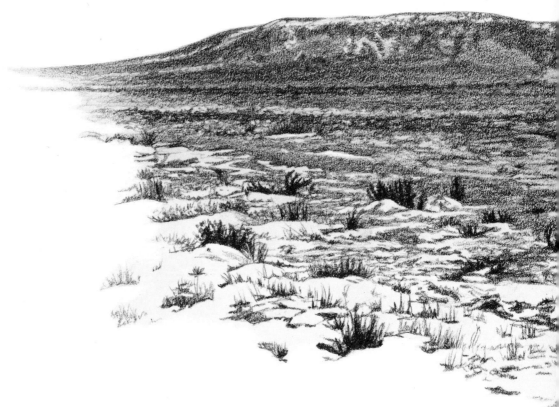

WINTER WINDMILL WITH EAGLE

"—that bird could be one of the eagles I used to see nesting on the cliffs above Turnagain Arm of Cook Inlet in Alaska."

"Yeah, Butch, but nobody really knows how far south Alaskan golden eagles migrate," Jack responded, calling me by the nickname that has persisted from my childhood.

"It was a day just like this when I saw a pair of eagles scare the hell out of three coyotes," he continued, changing the subject.

"Did they nab one?" I asked.

"No, but the coyotes sure knew they'd been chased."

Then Jack told me his favorite eagle-coyote story for the first time, one of his many experiences that I have heard him repeat at least once or twice a year ever since. I always listen for changes from one telling to the next, but never hear any, so I do not doubt his accuracy.

He and Dave Rogers, a mutual friend of ours who is also intrigued by raptors, saw two eagles flying in tandem across the grasslands ahead

of them and in the same direction they were driving. One, flying at about eighty feet, was just above and behind the other, over prairie crisscrossed at intervals by fences and shallow draws lined with fourwing saltbush. There the coyotes could find black-tailed jackrabbits, cottontails, deer mice, and other rodents.

Shortly, Jack and Dave spotted the coyotes running out of a draw and across the road a hundred yards ahead of them—ninety degrees away from the eagles' paths! The double threat of an approaching automobile and a pair of hunting eagles set the coyotes into a swift light-legged run.

Then, after the eagles turned to attack, great panicked strides carried the canines away much faster. Frequently they broke pace to jump across irregularities in the terrain and to glance at the ever-closer eagles.

I really did not want to hear the rest of Jack's story. Too many times before, in Alaska, George, Dave, and Bill came home with graphic accounts of gyrfalcons killing ptarmigan or of goshawks grabbing arctic hares. Why had I seen only one or two such events in the wild in my life? I blamed it on getting a formal education, a time-consuming undertaking that tends to keep one out of the field where the most personally satisfying lessons are to be learned. Still over a year away from my Ph.D., I felt a tug of despair that crisp morning. But mine were torments that everyone experiences now and then. Was it worth the time? The effort? The worry? Would the goals be reached?

Jack continued his story. The eagles' first tactic was to stoop on the last coyote in the group, raking their huge hind talons across its back. First one and then the other eagle struck, not really trying to grab onto the coyote, but rolling it over and giving it a good gash in the rump to slow it down. Each time before it was struck, the four-legged predator—now prey—yelped like an injured dog. Without concern for the delayed member of their pack, the other coyotes were then running far beyond a barbed-wire fence.

About fifteen yards from the fence, the larger eagle struck the tagalong and bound to it, lifting its hind legs off the ground with the momentum of the strike. The wailing coyote kept running on its front legs for a moment before the eagle let go to avoid colliding with the fence. The coyote's rump hit a strand of barbed wire that slung its body backward a few feet. But the coyote was tough. It landed virtually on its paws and immediately picked up its afflicted gait, haplessly trailing its companions, but spared by the eagles, which flew off, presumably to hunt weaker prey.

When Jack had completed relating this gem from his personal experience, the eagle sunbathing on the windmill suddenly seemed to become a symbol of rebuff. I saw myself as a tagalong, far behind many of my companions in the ageless enterprise of finding both adventure and solitude in the generous hands of nature. I felt like the animal being carried half off the ground, not knowing if the eagle of academia would let me go—with even as few scars as the real eagles had given the coyote. Would I suffer more than one impaling on barbed wire before being allowed to go my way? I saw only dreary weather ahead, with courses still to take and teach and with my thesis to write and defend.

Fifteen months later, alone and in very different circumstances, I was again on the prairie. The countryside was replete with an inspiring sharpness.

Intermittent snow driven by bitter-cold early-morning wind from the northwest left just a dusting of flakes upon the ground, enough to lend the wide-open spaces a light frosting below a cloudy but clearing sky. Winter wheat barely two inches high toward a mid-July harvest was rich green above snow trapped in the lee of shallow furrows plowed the preceding fall. The farmer's tractor path was revealed by fine green-and-white lines coursing together across the rolling hills, like green fingerprints on the whitest of paper. A few hundred feet north and south lay parallel lines of golden tan and white—last year's stubble, unplowed and stiff as whiskers above snow-bitten soil left fallow to collect the moisture of a year, a necessity of dry-land farming. Every snowfall, every rain shower must be garnered lest the next crop falter below summer's searing sun.

To the west, the foothills of the majestic Rocky Mountains were partially obscured by a squall of snow. In the foreground, a dry creek and a few fringing trees interrupted the expanse of cultivated land; a line of cliffs overlooked the wheat fields that lay in the shadows of clouds. These natural rumples in the prairie's skin were favors to wildlife, because the absence of intensive agriculture provided sanctuary for birds not adapted—and most are not—to nesting on the ground in new winter wheat or stubble. One such bird, an adult female golden eagle, sat motionless on a prominent rock atop the cliff; her mate soared overhead.

The sanctuary also benefited mammals whose gestation and suckling periods were too long to escape periodic burial of half their litters by the plow. A mile away, near where a road crossed the creek bed, a cottontail hopped into a wide band of wheat.

My discovery of the shortgrass prairie that morning changed to adventure only after I asked myself what the pastoral setting was telling me. Twenty-one years of formal education lay just hours behind, and many years of learning by choice lay ahead. I had successfully defended my dissertation. The eagle had released me, but it was like getting out of bed at eleven o'clock in the morning of my life. Ah—for the first time in years I could let myself enjoy spring fever! As a scientist by schooling, a naturalist by choice, and a falconer by inspiration, I found March's mix of tantalizing experiences appealing to my senses in a hundred ways. I had been to the prairie before, with Jack and with others, but never with time to savor each observation or without pressure from the demands of academic routine.

I do not remember reflecting on my past much that first day out, except for an uneasy feeling of "Isn't there something I should be studying?" No! They really had passed me the day before. Also, Dean Amadon, of the American Museum of Natural History, had called some time be-

fore to tell me that I was the recipient of a postdoctoral fellowship in their Department of Ornithology *if* I successfully completed my doctorate. Perhaps it was the double threat of not getting the degree and of losing the opportunity to study birds full time and without restraints for at least a year that made the last months of college so unbearable and the first days afield so memorable. I felt like a new world-heavyweight champion after winning a fifteen-round split decision, but having been almost knocked out several times in the closing rounds. What sticks with me now, fortunately, is the exhilaration of the morning after; I was puffy-eyed but clear-sighted, cut but not bleeding, and dazed but in full command of my victory.

March 16th had dawned in snow, but by midmorning the sun's rays frequently pierced heavy clouds to accent the beauty of grain fields, leafless trees in creek beds, and gentle east-facing slopes of prairie. Every fence post, tree, and bush was lightly rimed with a sparse stippling of snow.

I watched the perched eagle take flight from the cliff top and begin searching for lifting air currents, while her mate moved out of sight to the south. Air near the ground warmed and rose in large bubbles—called thermals—made visible by the female eagle climbing effortlessly, five hundred, seven hundred, and still many feet higher. She circled masterfully on the thermal's edge with wings as full as a schooner's sails in a steady wind, and my thoughts rode with her.

Her wingspread was nearly seven and a half feet, probably half a foot more than her mate's. The only distinctive feature of her underparts was the contrasting of her dark brown underwing and body feathers with her lighter brown and slightly barred wing and tail quills. Underneath and from a distance, she appeared simply as a large dark bird. Her wings were bent slightly at the wrists, halfway between her body and the tips. As she wheeled to stay in the thermal, she banked and showed the deep golden hackles of her nape and the equally golden leading edge of each wing. Her wings were wide through most of their length, yet the tips were slotted like an open hand. Long narrow points of the outermost primary feathers—the largest pinions of the wings—extended beyond wider portions of their bases, making the tips resemble fingers. Slotting increases the lift of each wing and helps cut turbulence caused by the bird slicing air. With sensitive and precise changes of the wing-slot spacing in response to natural air turbulence, she sailed along as fluidly as the air currents themselves.

Thus she soared, changing direction by subtly altering the positions

ADULT GOLDEN EAGLES

of her wings or, more often, by twisting her tail to catch the wind currents. She trimmed her own sails—skippered herself through the sea of air. At times she slipped smoothly sidewise: by positioning the leading edges of her wings a little to the right of the wind in her face, and tilting her tail down and to the right, the combination of forces pushed her to the right. Occasionally she turned her back to the air currents and sped rapidly windwayward a few hundred yards. When she turned to face her source of lift again, she was circling in a different thermal. She was fully endowed with beauty, with strength, and with skill; she had a feather for every wind.

Because of the brisk weather that March morning, the cottontail was eating its fill of wheat later than usual. The progressively warmer rays of the sun had stimulated it to seek food and to venture far from the roadside burrow. Vulnerability to predation was high in spite of the rabbit's ability to run, dodge, turn, hide, and utilize cover effectively.

The widening circles of the golden eagle brought it over the rabbit. Now motionless except for a twitching nose, crouched to hide, the rabbit watched the eagle. Its fur was held tight in apprehension; its eyes were fully open to the threatening silhouette; its legs were poised for thrust.

With the eagle directly overhead, but almost a thousand feet high, the cottontail made a critical mistake. It bolted toward the safety of its hole near the road, having to cross much wheatland before the eagle descended from its place of command. With ears back and tail bouncing, the rabbit sped through new wheat and stubble. Neither provided much cover in mid-March.

The eagle—still steady in the wind, head arched below her body to look straight down, and intently searching a wide swath of ground—noted the rabbit's first leap. Quickly she folded her wings and dropped several hundred feet at a forty-five-degree angle away from the rabbit, which was by then a third of the way home. Smoothly but swiftly the predator reversed directions in a wide arc and continued to fall at a steeper angle to a position directly above the fleeing rabbit. The prey was then halfway, and soon two-thirds of the way to safety. When the eagle was three hundred feet directly above her prey, she folded her wings completely, pulled them to her sides, and dropped from the sky like a dead weight.

The rabbit *almost* felt the walls of the hole scrape its sides as much of the momentum of the fourteen-pound eagle was effectively transferred to the rabbit. The prey was hit in the rear, bowled over, grasped, and carried a few feet as both skidded to a stop. A shadow soon overcame

the rabbit, but it was not the darkness of the burrow. One massive eagle foot engulfed its head. The other foot gripped the rabbit's hind legs near the back. Luckless furry feet fell limp. The last third of the way to the burrow was too far; death was the rabbit's only release. In fifteen minutes, the eagle had eaten.

So it is, day in and day out. And so the story of my favorite way of life began anew for me. Violently, you say? Not at all! The pendulum of nature swings—to the predators and to the prey—back and forth. The careless, inexperienced, and weak fall and die; their deaths are prerequisite to survival of the fittest. But there is no cruelty, no remorse, for those are distresses of men, not of eagles or rabbits. Life, after aeons of selection, can cope with temporary setbacks, for nature has the capacity to renew her resources. Another cottontail was in that field within a month, one that could beat the eagle to safety—like the coyote that kept running until the eagles gave up, and like me as I escaped to the prairie toward communion with wild living things.

2

HIS NEEDS
ARE
HIS MESSAGE

At one minute past eleven in the morning of my life, I began looking in earnest for potential but unknown nesting areas of birds of prey. There were many. No one, including myself, really anticipated how successful my searches for raptor nests would be.

Uppermost in my mind during the early explorations was obtaining the consent of landowners to study raptors on some large block of land—say, several hundred square miles—where I could come and go more or less as I pleased. I did not relish asking permission, because I expected to be refused. A few people in my circle had—selfishly, I suspect—perpetrated the myth that cattlemen were not receptive to having biologists or anyone else on their land, whatever their reasons. I was told that one had to spend some time on the range chewing the fat with the ranch hands, branding cattle, and repairing fences to cement good relations. Then, as the tommyrot went, if a fifth of whiskey was mustered at the proper moment, and if you could drink the rancher under the table, he would soften enough to let you go your way.

Being a teetotaler, I found that definitely not my style, and I had misgivings about walking to a ranch house with a bottle of booze held at arm's length in one hand and a poker for the branding fire in the other—especially in mid-March, when there were no calves to brand. I could clearly imagine the chosen cattleman of the plains, his dirty old jean jacket stiff as leather, his pants legs half stuffed into his high-topped boots, a chaw of tobacco distorting one cheek, his face sporting a four-day growth of whiskers, and his worn Stetson atop his head. I could also see his reaction upon being confronted by a bowlegged bird watcher from the university wearing a Chicago-mobster trench coat, double-knit pants with the legs hanging neatly outside shiny new cowboy boots, and a cheap alpine hat that belonged on the prairie as much as a pair of skis in late July.

I just could not play the part.

With my old ski jacket to replace the raincoat, with a different pair of pants, and without the alpine hat, I nonetheless counted a lot on my bowlegs to see me past the first rancher. Cowboys do get bowlegs from riding horses, do they not? Fortunately, not until after I had talked to the rancher did it occur to me that I had never been on a horse.

It was soon obvious that I had been misled. The rancher was much as I had envisioned him, but his temperament was not. I found nearly every cattleman not only receptive to my plans but also willing to help by giving tips about the habits and whereabouts of raptors. They really did keep track of birds of prey, especially golden eagles.

One rancher, in particular, made an immediate success of my initial searches by telling me of a small stone observation hut overlooking an eagle nest on a piece of distant property that had been in his family since the turn of the century. Carrying his directions, which began at a small reservoir over seventy miles from my home, I journeyed to the blind for the first time on March 18th, a warm day of over sixty degrees in the afternoon, and quite a change from two days before.

Strong gusts of wind pushed across Antelope Reservoir (as I later came to call it) and up a grassy slope scattered with sagebrush, prickly pear, and yucca. Below the brittle blades of the previous year's growth, small, succulent shoots of blue grama and buffalo grass barely pierced the nearly continuous mat of these short, warm-season sod grasses. The cool-season grasses—those which develop most before summer arrives— were well started. Patches of Indian ricegrass, needle-and-thread grass, and western wheatgrass stood even higher than winter wheat in nearby fields. Yucca and prickly pear appeared much as they did at any other time of the year except when blooming. Most small birds were hidden behind bushes and rocks, grounded by the wind. Only horned larks, buffeted by prairie winds the year round, were unperturbed by the gusts.

I drove to the crest of the slope where each gust broke into visible turbulence over the small dirt road that had been made by early settlers and was now used by ranchers and their numerous cattle. Wisps of sand chased rolling tumbleweeds down the trail in a whirling path. The sand passed under a barbed-wire gate stretched across the road below a small cliff. The weeds joined others of their kind straining against the wire to continue their windswept journey. Most were trapped until the wind changed direction; only those held by the gate would eventually be unbound by the rancher passing to check his herds.

Through the gate was another pasture and another fence in the distance to catch the weeds—or was it the same fence?—parceling the land according to the design of today's ranchers. From the top of the cliff, where I parked on another trail due north of the eyrie—still following my informant's scribbled path—I gazed at seemingly unending strands of wire, always three high, strung west over a small hill and down to a dry creek and beyond, stretching straight for the horizon over smooth undulations of prairie. To the south, distant fence posts fused into a continuous line. Eastward the fence ended snug against the cliffs: the Eagle Breaks, a series of sixty-foot bluffs marking the transition from outwash of the Rocky Mountains up to the High Plains. Another fence began at the top of the Breaks and continued east.

HORNED LARK

I still had not seen an eagle. Perhaps the nest would be empty that year. My turn for one of the ups of being a naturalist was overdue. As I crawled the last eighty feet to the blind, in accordance with my directions, I harbored the fear of one more miss, yet I tingled with anticipation.

I dragged myself slowly through a small opening in the rear of the blind and looked cautiously over the edge of the peephole. An eagle was there! It must be the female, I thought. I was awed by her size, her air of greatness, and seeming omnipotence! Below her were thousands of acres of land virtually in her clutch. But she did not even glance at the blind; it had ceased to be a threat to her.

While I treasured the first good look at her, the wind increased noticeably. The whistles and hisses of its dash through the wires and across the face of the sandstone-and-conglomerate cliff were broken by distant rumblings of thunder. What a setup for watching eagles—and for getting wet! I could see light through cracks in the roof of the blind, and sharp blasts of wind eddied through the gaping door, seeking my limited shelter. The Eagle Breaks were in for another bit of sculpting at the weather's hand. The runoff would join the wind and sand in eroding the twenty-five-million-year-old cap rock of the cliff. A fierce gust bit the rock and pushed into every cavity and crevice as the sun faded behind the smooth leading edge of a rapidly approaching storm cloud.

The sky darkened, and the eagle's eyes closed wincingly to the bluster and first raindrops. She settled deeper into her nest, or eyrie, and presented her shallowest profile to foil the chill. With her head low, she could no longer see, as I could, the small, leafless trees immediately below her, or the broken foundation of an abandoned farmstead not a hundred feet to her left—for which this nest, the Foundation Eyrie, was named. Relics of the time when settlers lived below the cliff were nearly gone. All that remained were a few short sections of a foundation and the skeleton of a wooden door collapsed into a stone-lined ice cellar. The rancher's mother, whom I had met briefly, had eaten many cool desserts made with ice from that cellar. I wish now that I had talked more with her to learn of early life on the plains.

The eagle faced the wind conscious perhaps only through the faint coercion of instinct of the greater shelter that her alternate nest sites would have provided. I later found two such nests farther east along the Breaks. Both faced south or southwest, with their "backs" more to the prevailing winds; but some of her species nested farther west than in previous years, too close to these substitute sites, a fact I discovered later the same day. Apparently, after earlier nonviolent jostling of territorial boundaries between the pairs—a behavior I have never seen—she and her mate had repaired the sequestered nest by the deserted homestead.

Rain fell for less than fifteen minutes. The eagle, in fulfillment of a motherly solicitude, lay close over her nest after the storm, leaving me unsure of its contents. Beads of water rolled from her back, and each collected several other drops before all were splattered over the edge of the nest cup. She continued to shake raindrops from her head with annoyed, nodding motions. The rock overhang above her did not fend off rain driven by winds from the northwest.

She had an unrestricted view of the prairie to the south when she sat erect, and she kept idle visual contact with an unknowing coyote that moved away below the Breaks. The coyote, heavy with pups, had sought shelter from the storm two hundred yards north in what was to become her den. The eagle watched the coyote until it was over a mile away, reappearing only atop each of the undulations of prairie. Even the stealth of a coyote is not secret.

The coyote has stood up well to man's direct and vigorous persecution and has even defied active control programs. Some, mainly naturalists, find solace in that fact. Others, like sheep ranchers, are infuriated by the pesky creature and hold no less than a death wish for the entire species. My feelings are mixed. I do not side with such sheep ranchers, who, fortunately, were almost nonexistent near the Eagle Breaks. Nor do I find complete satisfaction in the coyote's success. To persevere, it has become a fugitive; its predatory life-style has been reversed. At times, cowardice is the coyote's only rescue, escape its only preoccupation. Every coyote I saw near the Eagle Breaks that also saw me was running away, often a bit sidewise to keep me in view. If I stopped the truck, it would straighten out and run faster.

Some call this cleverness or adaptability, but I could do without such adaptations. The response of a man upon seeing a fleeing coyote should be compassion. We are the last link in a long chain, and we are being shown our true identity. Man, the ultimate predator, makes prey of the coyote, and the terror-driven critter knows it. But I loathe being his predator. I would rather be something he chases—but rarely catches!—so that he would come looking for me, and I would be forced to know him better.

The brief rain was heavy; sand no longer shifted, yet water stood in only a few places. The crush of tumbleweeds was relaxed against the fence, for the wind had slackened behind the eastward-moving storm. Fertile soil below the cliff could have accepted ten times the water that fell. With that kind of generous dousing, the prairie could produce more grass than the cattle could subsequently consume. Such is not the norm, however. In the arid shortgrass prairie, less than fifteen inches of rain falls in an average year.

After ten or fifteen minutes, the eagle stood up momentarily and I could see two eggs—new life before the onset of spring.* As I continued to enjoy this long-awaited treat, the male eagle appeared over the hill to the northwest, unaware of my watchful eyes peering from behind binoculars in the blind. Probably having weathered the rain in a large cottonwood tree near Antelope Reservoir, he was returning with a freshly killed rabbit. Despite the encumbrance of the two-pound cottontail slung below his eight or nine pounds, he accomplished his arrival on the cliff, between me and the nest, gracefully and skillfully. He could have carried two such rabbits, although not much more than that.

The female eagle stayed over her eggs, but watched her mate closely. She was noticeably larger than the tiercel (as most male birds of prey are called). Unfortunately, the size difference was not always apparent when each was alone; indeed, determining the sex of live eagles is difficult because the size and weight of the sexes overlap. My colleagues grumble incessantly about this shortcoming in their expertise.

---

*Golden eagles lay eggs before the first day of spring only in the southern part of their breeding range. In total, their range encompasses Eurasia above the tropics, including also the northwest corner of Africa, and North America except for the Mexican tropics. Specific areas within this vast breeding range that do not support nesting golden eagles are: (1) the United States east of the North Dakota-to-Texas corridor of states (except for a few pairs in the Appalachian Mountains), (2) Switzerland and other parts of central Europe, (3) west-central Asia (where golden eagles are replaced by several other species of the genus *Aquila*, such as the greater and lesser spotted eagles, imperial eagles, and tawny eagles), (4) the northern several hundred miles of Russia, (5) most of the Canadian mainland northwest of Hudson Bay, and (6) all the Canadian arctic islands, Greenland, and Iceland.

Thus, in the southern portions of their breeding range—for example, in Mexico, the Middle East, and Morocco—golden eagles deposit eggs in January and February. In more temperate regions, such as the western United States,

For me, however, beginning with a fifty-fifty chance of being right, and using the old falconers' impression that female raptors are larger, broader-shouldered, and have relatively more massive feet, thicker tarsi, larger heads, and larger beaks than their mates, I am content in being right a high percentage of the time, if not always. Added to this are the differences in behavior during the nesting period. Alas! Let me contend with academia.

At the Foundation Eyrie, the female's thirteen or fourteen pounds *did* provide her with a slightly broader and taller stature than her mate's. She and others like her rank in size with other birds of prey in North America below only California condors and, possibly, the large bald eagles of Alaska. And her mate *did* have a smaller head, less massive feet, and the look of a tiercel, evidenced, in large part, by subtle behavioral expressions, mannerisms, and poise.

The tails of golden eagles—hers nearly sixteen inches long and marbled with diffuse wisps of tan—are lighter brown than their backs. Their flanks and tarsi are covered, completely to their toes, with short, light brown feathers. This led to the term "booted eagles" for golden eagles and kindred species throughout the world.

About half of the almost sixty species of eagles in the world are booted eagles. The golden eagle is the only booted eagle found in America north of Mexico, and the only eagle of the genus *Aquila* in the New World. A fine one it is, though; we are fortunate to have it in our midst. Seeing their size, strength, and boldness at close range at the Foundation Eyrie made me appreciate more than before why eagles fly high in the symbolic creations of artists, the beautiful metaphors of poets, and the lofty ideas of many philosophers. Too bad these positive aspects are only slightly more prevalent than the myths, malice, and mysteries that, in the absence of knowledge, have grown apace in the minds of some farmers, ranchers, hunters, and others who oppress eagles and other predatory animals for supposed personal gain. But that is material for a different book.

Scotland, and east-central Asia, most eggs are laid during March and April. Across much of Canada, along the fjords and in the higher forests of Scandinavia, throughout much of the Russian interior, and in the mountains of Alaska, golden eagles lay in April and early May. In south-central Alaska, I have found eggs in golden eagle eyries in June. In the Alaskan, Canadian, and Scandinavian arctic, the northernmost parts of the range, eggs are sometimes *laid* that late.

The three other types of eagles in the world include four species of snake eagles, four harpy eagles, and ten sea eagles. Snake eagles occur only in the Old World. As their name suggests, serpents are their primary food. Most are small to medium-sized eagles, not much larger than the red-tailed hawk, a common North American soaring hawk. The word "eagle" does not always imply large size.

Among the harpy eagles, on the other hand, are some of the world's largest birds of prey. All live in the tropical forests of New Guinea, the Philippines, Mexico, and Central and South America. They are the most formidable of aerial predators.

The bald eagle, the national bird of the United States, is a sea eagle. It is an uncommon bird near the Eagle Breaks, present only in winter. The two eagles of North America are not very closely related; each is at the end of a different line of evolution in the family of birds known as the Accipitridae. This family includes all kites, hawks, eagles, and Old World vultures.

The bald eagle gets its name from the white plumage of the heads of adults; their tails are also white. Many who know the aggressive ways of golden eagles look upon bald eagles as lackluster scavengers. I have seen them disturb a gull colony off Kodiak Island, in Alaska, every few minutes to steal a gull chick as food for eagle chicks at a nest on the mainland. Bald eagles also patrol salt-water beaches, riverbanks, and lake shores, looking for dead or dying fish and other animal remains. In the absence of an easily obtained meal, however, they can catch their own live fish, pirate one from an osprey, or actively pursue full-grown waterfowl, gulls, rabbits, and other animals when and where the circumstances dictate.

Thus, Benjamin Franklin was partially, but not wholly, justified almost two centuries ago in suggesting that the North American turkey would be a more reputable symbol of a vigorous new nation. In a letter to Sarah Bache, Franklin lamented:

> I wish the bald eagle had not been chosen as the representative of our country; he is a bird of bad moral character; like those among men who live by sharping and robbing, he is generally poor, and often very lousy.

I am quite happy Franklin lost his bid, because without laws protecting bald eagles, which have been encouraged by the symbolism, there would certainly be fewer eagles today, both balds and goldens. This book might then have been a pessimistic account of the golden eagle's future.

But there was no reason for pessimism at the Foundation Eyrie. Its occupants and their surroundings, all freshened by the passing storm and then brightened by the sun's reappearance, stood like a vibrant painting designed from my anticipatory dreams during the preceding months. What a setting for golden eagles! Bird songs, smells of spring air cleansed by rain, the wide-open spaces, and the chill of rain-drenched clothes assailed all my senses at once. I responded by shivering less—or, at least, I did not think about the dampness as my consciousness attempted to sort out nature's stimulants. Too few people have ever experienced, so closely and so completely free of the pangs of day-to-day living, the warming solitude of an eagle nest.

Yet my problem was different. I was free to savor the enrichment of many such experiences; and my education allowed greater depth in analyzing behaviors, appreciating the complexity of bird song, identifying and counting the prey at an eagle nest, and writing technical papers. I am happy to have such skills, but the book learning also constrains me. Little can be left to the imagination. My schooling requires me to seek relationships and reasons, causes and effects, and then to draw conclusions.

Does the eagle hear other birds? Does he know the freshness of March from the harshness of December—in July? Perhaps the poet would be a better judge. I must look at him too technically to feel the embrace of a warm breeze as he does—if he does! Does an eagle ever smell the sage? The rain? The cattle? Does he "enjoy" a prairie morning? Perhaps in the freedom of imagination others can experience the golden sunrise exactly like an eagle, but I cannot.

In the center of the vibrant scene was the nest, a large platform of sticks up to two inches in diameter, neatly stacked on a slightly overhung ledge. It was topped with a nearly complete ring of light brown shredded yucca root and dead yucca spears. An occasional green yucca plant had been built in or flattened onto the surface around a nest cup lined with smaller yucca spears and dry grass. Among the sticks were several cow ribs and a large leg bone, all bleached white by years of exposure to the sun. Even short pieces of barbed wire had found their way to the nest in the eagles' beaks. Antlers of small deer often appear in eagle nests, as do burlap bags, rags, newspapers, stockings, and other litter.

Below the nest, on the bare rock of the vertical cliff, small, bright orange lichens colored the stone. Certain lichens apparently derive some necessary nutrient from the whitewash or excrements of birds, enabling the lowly plants to live on the austere provisions of rocks. Soil below the nest supported several grasses and other plants more characteristic of the prairie to the south than of the ground under the cliff. Seeds brought by the eagles, particularly cheatgrass and Russian thistle seeds adhering to prey of years past, drop to the ground and germinate. During the growing season, some eagle nests can be pinpointed from afar if one notices such unusual clumps of plants.

Within four feet of the bulky accumulation of sticks were dozens of mud nests of cliff swallows glued under a small overhang. All were in various states of disrepair, with entrances worn by wind and rain to several times the normal size for swallows. They were mere foundations, like the pioneers' house below the bluff. Many cliff nests of raptors in the West have swallow colonies nearby, partly for protection afforded the smaller birds by large, predatory birds two to three hundred times their weight, and partly just because there is an overhang available. The swallows were still weeks away, just preparing to leave their Central and South American wintering grounds.

Other birds nest among the very sticks of eagle nests. A pair of house sparrows were already constructing a nest deep within the Foundation Eyrie to take advantage of the sanctuary of a bird sufficiently large to defend against most mammalian predators, but too large to catch small, agile sparrows and swallows. The animation of sparrows flitting in and out with small pieces of dry grass enhanced the charm of the nest scene.

On top of the cliff, in the foreground a little to the left of the eyrie, was the rabbit, its shiny winter coat showing no evidence of shedding. It was held down by the tiercel eagle's bright yellow feet, each toe tipped with a sharp black talon buried half an inch in fur and flesh. I could hear him rip the flesh and crack small bones with a sharply hooked, steel-black beak that protruded at its base from a fleshy yellow cere. His tools were finely honed and effective; he plied a good knife and fork, both in the quantity of food eaten and in the expediency of doing so.

His deep brown eyes searched the fare for easy bites, but often shifted to his incubating mate or to something outside my visual range. Perhaps the coyote was still busy gleaning a meal from the prairie, or a passing marsh hawk was doing the same. Golden eagles are said to have eight-power eyes, although no one really knows. Whatever their ability, I must use blinds and good optics—spotting scopes, binoculars, and telephoto lenses—to compete in the world of farsighted birds of prey.

The spotting scope is the key tool of my favorite brand of bird study. Much field work involves just surveying raptor populations and determining nesting successes. For that, mountaineering equipment and tree-climbing spikes are in order, though a scope saves miles of walking by bringing trees and cliffs closer.

I cling to the most intimate contacts with raptors; memories of their private lives stay with me the longest. To appreciate such observations fully, one especially needs a point of view acceptable to both the birds and the naturalist. The scope does not just make distant observation easier; it is an equalizer that takes the visual advantage of raptors away from them. It gives me a privileged placement, like the one given here in a very different way. What a pity we must accomplish with cold metal and glass—or paper and pen—what an eagle does with its miraculous eyes.

Finally, the male eagle stepped off the kill and flew to the nest. His mate left gracefully, circled out over the trail, and then flew back to the cottontail. Her movements reflected rays of sun from golden hackles. Both were beautifully crowned—golden eagles, the King and Queen of Birds, *Aquila chrysaëtos*, common, figurative, and scientific names, respectively, given them by early ornithologists and Linnaeus to establish their regal and technical positions among all birds.

Less than a hundred feet from me was a type of excellence recognized by Aristotle three hundred and fifty years before the coming of Christ; by kings such as Henry VII, who, by decree, reserved eagles for an emperor's recreation during the heyday of falconry in the Middle Ages; and by many of today's naturalists—amateur and professional—whose store of knowledge not available to Aristotle allows ever more appreciation of natural things.

I remember asking myself many questions while sitting in the blind at the Foundation Eyrie. "If I had Aristotle's wisdom, Henry VII's power and unlimited finances, and today's technology and leisure, what could I do for golden eagles?" The question was presumptuous, but there was only one answer: everyone must see the beauty of an eagle's flight and feel the chill of finality in an eagle's pursuit of prey; and everyone must understand the complexity of an eagle's biological needs.

The eagle's needs are his message to mankind, because where an eagle can breathe, procreate, and roam, so can man! Clearly, a place must be made for eagles so that we may withstand the test of time with them.

3

A LONG AND INTERESTING HISTORY

By the time the female eagle at the Foundation Eyrie returned to her eggs, and I could leave without disturbing her, the gloss of moisture on nearby rocks had dulled and the chocolate brown of wet soil had faded several shades toward its usual dusty hue. I expected the gumbo to cling to my boots like clay as I retraced my path to the truck, but the water had evaporated and soaked in rapidly. Even my clothes had dried, probably just from the warmth of my excitement.

My thoughts turned to the days ahead as I drove a few hundred yards back west and then slowly south along a rutted trail running below the Breaks. It took me past the Foundation Eyrie, but I stopped only to open and close the barbed-wire gate. I could barely see the low profile that the eagle presented as though I were another threatening storm cloud. Since I had pressed my luck far enough by sneaking to the blind, I wanted to leave her without suspicions. Apparently it worked: my passing did not make her flee.

With the Foundation Eyrie and a complaisant rancher as lures, the Eagle Breaks showed strong promise as an intensive study area where I could come and go more as weather permitted, rather than at the whim of the unaccommodating ranchers I still expected to find.

My thoughts about the future centered on the fact that all the inside information I had possessed, like the rancher's tip about the Foundation Eyrie, had come to an end. I had no more knowledge of other eagle nests. I was on my own. It was not only my turn to enjoy what I saw, but also my task to seek out new and engaging natural events. My major professor in graduate school had often forecast for his students the loneliness of professional life, emphasizing that individual pride of accomplishment follows from one's own initiative, not from the enterprise of others. Independence was his lesson, more so than how animals function internally, how they behave, or how well they integrate themselves into their environment. Zoology was merely his vehicle for the personal development of his students.

Having the burden of production—of testing what I had learned—squarely on my shoulders was an unusual feeling. It was not only a fresh sensation, like seeing my first hawk or learning an important new fact about the Breaks, but also a feeling of renewal, which showed in the first impressions of the Eagle Breaks recorded in my field notebook. Later, I was surprised at the truth of these early words written amid pages of technical notes:

> It is difficult to imagine the history of this area, not only through man's eyes but from the bird's viewpoint as well. Each year—each windy, rainy, and stormy year—the falling bluffs fold decades of human habitation and millennia of avian life under tons of rock and fine silt. And then runoffs from spring rains carry everything south onto the rolling grasslands, which bear witness to the passage of time, to the deaths of stately cliffs, and to the evolution of their wildlife.

Many months passed before I realized the pertinence of those early impressions. I subsequently read at length about the geology, prehistoric animals, and, especially, the human history of the western Great Plains in order to understand better the ecology of birds of prey near the Eagle Breaks. Many questions arose. When and how were the Breaks formed? When and from where did man immigrate into the area? How has man influenced birds of prey through the centuries?

The geologic history of the Eagle Breaks was important to me because golden eagles more often nest on cliffs than in trees. Prairie falcons nest almost exclusively on ledges and in cavities of sheer rock or dirt palisades. Before the Breaks were formed, when the western Great Plains were more uniform than they are today, cliff-nesting raptors were either absent from the area or restricted to riverbanks, or had different nesting instincts. Golden eagles and prairie falcons probably nested more in the fastnesses of the Rocky Mountains, which still awaited a third and last great uplift to their current heights.

Five million years ago, most Rocky Mountain peaks were as much as thirty-five hundred feet lower than they are today. The titanic skyward movements of billions of tons of rock increased not only the rain-catching power of the mountains but also the velocity of streams. Water was channeled eastward along the lines of least resistance, through canyons opening onto the plains, while the prairies turned drier in the rain shadow of the growing mountains.

Immediately below the Rockies, as far as seventy-five miles east of the Front Range, rapidly flowing water swept the soils and sediments of the High Plains into large rivers flowing still farther east, eventually to the Gulf of Mexico via the Missouri and Mississippi Rivers. The demarcation between the inundated land and the untouched High Plains surface is represented today by hundreds of miles of cliffs, called "breaks" by the people who live near them. The breaks persist today and serve as nest sites for birds of prey because the exposed cap rock is durable yet extensively pockmarked with nooks and crannies produced by continuous, slow erosion. The rolling grasslands do in fact bear witness to the passage of time and to the passing of stately cliffs.

The history of man near the Eagle Breaks is of great interest to me because he is new and potentially dangerous to eagles. Almost since their evolution—which in sequence was millions of years before men came—golden eagles have nested in the forests and on the cliffs of North America without interference from man. Prehistoric men immigrated to this continent from Siberia across the Bering land bridge sometime between twelve and twenty thousand years ago: the precise time is much debated by archaeologists. Considering the suddenness of man's influx—in terms of evolutionary time—it is surprising that golden eagles have not gone the way of mammoths, camels, and now extinct species of bison that were present when man first came.

But fortunately early men sought food, the large mammals; predators were too elusive. I cannot say, however, that the Asian newcomers and their descendants did not molest eagles. As hunters and gatherers, they probably ate whatever they could catch. Just by climbing a tree or reaching with a spear, they could steal food brought to young raptors by their parents. Prehistoric men may have been the first practitioners

BADGERS IN DISPUTE

of raptor conservation by employing raptors, at least temporarily, as providers during the nesting season—instead of killing them! In the end, however, a tasty repast of raptor "squab" might have finished the arrangement, all for naught as far as conservation goes.

It must have taken me over two hours to search the first three miles of cliff—during what I had planned to be a quick reconnaissance just to become acquainted with the extent of the Eagle Breaks. I had discovered the two alternate eagle nests, but was becoming disappointed at not finding another active site. A fleeting glance at a prairie falcon whetted my anticipations, but the falcon showed no attraction to any potential nest site. Nor did my theoretical knowledge of bird territories serve me well, because my impatience put an eagle nest on every ledge. The scope righted my wrongs time after time, to my chagrin.

I was surprised at one point in my search to come across two bad-gers, apparently in a brief territorial encounter. The badger hole — a den, judging from the time of year and the length of time it was later oc-cupied — was less than fifty feet from the trail. The full-grown predators, each weighing over twenty pounds, were engaged in a nose-to-nose stand-off near the hole. Unfortunately, as soon as I stopped the truck, one left the fray and the other went down the burrow; I surmised that the resident female was running off another female or a passing male. I am still puzzled at having seen those mostly nocturnal creatures above ground by day.

When I first saw them, their stances were typical of the reaction each would have to a man: crouched on their forefeet ready to attack, noses wrinkled, lips curled to show the teeth, and hair erect — especially the long hair on their sides, which made them appear much larger than normal. They hiss and strike at a man, but at every chance they turn tail and almost slither through the grass in retreat, as the interloper here did on being confronted by the resident. It seemed to drag its belly across the prairie, but its short legs managed remarkable speed.

Around the burrow, dirt was piled but not scattered about the surface. On subsequent visits, I saw that small amounts of new dirt had appeared above ground—apparent housecleaning to keep soil from filling the den. The round hole was always open to the surface, but it soon became oval-shaped underground, about twelve inches wide and eight inches high. This conforms to the shape of the badger's somewhat flattened body. The actual tunnel may be only three or four inches tall, but loose soil lies several inches deep on the floor. The badger reaches forward and scrapes the dirt underneath itself, where the hind feet collect it and expel it behind the animal. The result is forward propulsion, usually faster than one man can follow digging with a hand shovel.

I later found eagle predation on such medium-sized mammalian predators to be uncommon. I have only once seen a badger even listed as prey of golden eagles in North America. Several coyote kills, mostly pups, have been recorded; and bobcats, raccoons, and foxes are taken on occasion. Skunks and weasels, because they are smaller, are killed more often, but account for only about one-hundredth of all golden eagle prey recorded in the United States. In general, it is as difficult for eagles to find small mammalian predators to eat as it is for naturalists to observe them.

The trail I was following, after deteriorating for three miles, passed a windmill and then swung closer to the cliff. If one seeks peace on the plains nowadays, one arrives by means of grass-filled ruts, the sign of low traffic flow. The trail led me to a point where the entire precipice overhung the ground by as much as twenty feet. I later learned that sheltered areas like this one had been occupied by men during at least seven lengthy periods, including the times of early mammoth and bison hunters.

Much later, between A.D. 1200 and 1870, Indians from some or all of the Pawnee, Apache, Comanche, Arapaho, and, finally, Cheyenne tribes lived under or frequented the huge slanting overhangs of stone that run for over a hundred feet along the cliff. The cliff-formed lean-tos open to the south, away from the prevailing winds, and still supply water within their cover from the seepage of two small springs.

I was attracted to the ancient dwellings by two tiny caves about eighty feet apart at the tip of the overhang—in the upper lip of the

gaping cliff. Each hole was about three feet in diameter, two or more feet deep, and whitewashed below with the excrements of either wood rats or raptors. It was a dandy spot for prairie falcons, but when I focused the spotting scope carefully, the only feathers I saw were the ear tufts and head of a great horned owl. I wondered if owls had nested there when elephant hunters and Indians inhabited the shelters.

I left the owl in its retreat and drove around a prominent point of the cliff line. At first I was awed by several more miles of bluffs ahead of me, but my attention was quickly drawn to the most whitewash I have ever seen on a cliff. It ran two feet down and six feet along the cliff below a small ledge. I scoped the ledge, which was sharply overhung by three or four feet of rock, but it was too narrow even for a prairie falcon eyrie. Nor would wood rats spend enough time on such a naked ledge to color the stone so creamy white.

After later finding a prairie falcon eyrie a little over a mile west, I concluded that the ledge was a wintering perch for the falcons and that they had gone elsewhere to nest. Their departure may have been hastened by a pair of golden eagles, the first I found by myself near the Eagle Breaks.

At the left end of the overhang, I spotted a pile of sticks capped with a thin, dark mass; I had learned in Alaska that that meant an eagle was present. There is an extra thrill in finding a nest that, as far as you know, no one else has ever seen.

Feeling like a kid who has just found a ten-dollar bill, I departed the Indian Eyrie—as we later called it, because of the nearby stone shelters. I wanted to climb to get a closer look, but it was too late in the day. Had I bumped the incubating bird off, it might not have returned before nightfall, and that was the last thing I wanted.

I called it a day at that point and drove back to the windmill I had passed earlier. There I fought the cattle for a drink of cool water as the sun fell beneath a layer of clouds that hung over the Rockies. The rays came in almost horizontally and highlighted the long line of rock just north of me. The lowing of cattle seemed to welcome nighttime. At last, they could lie down, cease filling their cavernous stomachs, and chew their cuds.

The cattle days near the Eagle Breaks began in the mid-1800s, with large drives of cattle up the Goodnight-Loving Trail from Texas to Montana. The Indians, who would never have exhausted the plant and animal life of the Great Plains, finally vacated the surrounding wild country under pressure from white men. It took the white man's slaughter of buffalo, ranching, settling, and farming to bring about the much altered conditions of today. The years from 1875 to 1890 produced a devastating assault on the buffalo economy of the Plains Indian, in preparation for a new mode of land use, cattle ranching. During the 1860s, the great cattle baron John Wesley Iliff gradually gained control of the water for hundreds of miles around the Eagle Breaks. He turned five hundred dollars into a million between 1856 and 1881. The cattle business flourished for less than a decade more, until the disastrous winters of the late 1880s.

The coming of homesteaders and farmers during the 1890s and after ushered in still another era. Man's interference with eagle nests then increased owing to sheer numbers of people. But early settlement and farming of the non-irrigable shortgrass and mixed-grass prairie were cheerless failures. Attempts to domesticate the prairie were bankrupt before the settlers boarded trains in Chicago or spread toward the prairie from arable land near large rivers.

As my explorations of the countryside around the Eagle Breaks spanned years of history and hundreds of miles, I passed the dregs of dry-farming pioneers who had made a desperate but futile stand against the elements. Forty or eighty or a hundred and sixty acres of dry-land crops just would not support a family, except under ideal conditions. Lack of rain was the critical, defeating factor. Yet the human tide advanced, and by 1915 only the least desirable acreages—sandhills, breaks, and pebble-strewn ridges—were left for homesteading. Cattle ranches were reduced in size. Sodbusters, squatters, nesters—call them what you wish—controlled the rest.

The new residents of the prairie broke the original sod to plant wheat, alfalfa, corn, millet, rye, barley, and potatoes. With horses and plows, and later tractors, the prairie was drawn and quartered, laid defenseless against the wind. Farmers set the charge and nature detonated it. The result was the dust bowl, the most widespread ecological disaster in recent North American history. Some pioneers survived their ordeal; others did not. The house below the Foundation Eyrie, for example, was occupied for nearly four decades, but the rancher's mother's family was driven out by drought and blowing dust during the thirties.

Ironically, many of the once-fenced homesteads of sodbusters—the scourge of men like John Iliff, who fought to keep cattle ranges open—have now reverted to pastureland. Today, Black Angus and Hereford cattle graze the shortgrasses much as did Texas longhorns years ago and bison before them. We may never see bison, cougars, elk, wolves, grizzlies, and other extirpated animals roaming freely on the plains again, but we can, as I learned to do, appreciate what remains, what has returned, and how the present conditions came about, with the fervent hope that some areas will revert ever closer to original conditions.

While I was driving home that evening, first nearly blinded by the setting sun and then with vision dimmed by darkness, I contemplated ways of finding every raptor nest on the Breaks. I was not satisfied with my once-over-lightly, even though I must have stopped every two hundred feet to glass the cliff. It seemed that raptors could nest in any of a thousand nooks and crannies in each mile of bluffs. Checking every pigeonhole for a pigeon, so to speak, was a slow process.

The thought of pigeons sent me back over twelve years to my first significant leanings toward raptor study. I must have mulled those beginnings over and over for fifty miles on the way home, because they were as incredible as a sheep rancher suddenly falling in love with coyotes and offering them his fold as a fee for some sort of deliverance.

As a fourteen-year-old, I worshiped the small flock of racing pigeons I owned. With the fifty dollars a month I earned from my paper route, I had built a large pigeon coop, imported a flock of sixteen classy blue-bars and blue-checks from California to Alaska, and bought my first twenty-dollar book, Wendell M. Levi's *The Pigeon*. I remember hours of fascinated reading about the different breeds of pigeons of the world as depicted in that definitive work of the time. Unfortunately, when it came time for the first eggs to hatch in my loft, a much anticipated event, I was in the hospital. I missed the very first dynamic happening along my path to becoming a staunch ally of nature.

That same spring, my friend George acquired a young red-tailed hawk that had fallen from its nest prematurely. This was years before the ventures to Goodnews Bay and Mount McKinley National Park. I forget the details of the young hawk, but Chirpy Bird, as it was jokingly named, aroused my interest and started a series of accidents and, later, purposeful decisions that led me to the Eagle Breaks.

As things turned out, though, the pigeons, my homelife, and a gyrfalcon played more important roles than Chirpy Bird in determining my subsequent priorities. My mother and father were (and still are) amateur radio operators. One whole room of our small house was crammed with the best equipment they could muster, and in the back yard stood a fifty-foot steel antenna tower with a comfortable sitting platform just below the top. During my pigeon-raising days, I climbed my ladder to the sky almost daily to look out at my homers exercising about the neighborhood.

One morning before school, as I sat in the watchtower enjoying the beauty of autumn's first snow on the Chugach Mountains and watching the pigeons racing above the treetops, I heard a jingling sound that grew louder and louder, and finally joined the whistle of pigeon wings in the sky. A gyrfalcon suddenly passed through the flock, scattering them widely. Then it grabbed one of my expensive California imports and fluttered to the ground across the street between a house and a garage.

I never did remember climbing down the tower in my haste to save the pigeon, nor did I think about the long history of unfriendly behavior exhibited by the residents of the house. Cold, perplexed stares bore down on me from the neighbors' breakfast window as I rushed into their yard to scare the falcon away. I was fifteen feet away when I stopped suddenly, realizing that the bells meant it was a trained bird. I dropped to a crawl before moving in more slowly, as I had seen George do with Chirpy Bird. Besides, there was no need for haste; the prey had heard the jingle of its death bells, one of which was hanging delicately on each leg of the predator. The falcon was also outfitted with leather straps or jesses, the accouterments of falconry, an ancient art in which wild birds of prey are trained to hunt in companionship with man and his dogs.

As the fate of my flock would have it, that gyrfalcon had been meticulously taught to chase pigeons. Its tenacity at the sport had led to its truancy: it simply flew out of its falconer's control in pursuit of a strong-flying pigeon. Unfortunately mine were not so strong. Cajoling my way, I got to within three feet of the falcon's jesses, but the bird suddenly left me kneeling over a dead pigeon; then it circled up over the tower, flew down another of my feathered pets, and carried it waveringly toward a nearby pond.

At that point, I informed my mother school would have to wait a day, and then I phoned George to come and help me capture the falcon. He soon arrived from five blocks away, panting and red-faced from having run every step. Later I wished I had not called him.

"Where's the bird? What kind is it? Get me a pigeon!" He was shouting with excitement and promptly took over the operation, even though he knew we would have to return the falcon to its owner.

"What do you mean get a pigeon?" I asked. "It's got all my pigeons it's gonna get!"

The gyrfalcon had found an easy source of food, and George was determined to keep him well-fed—at my expense! Two days and six more pigeons later—eight altogether, mind you—George and the gyrfalcon finally got together. The slaughter was not brought about because the bird wanted to kill all my pigeons; it was because George kept interrupting its meals in trying to snare it. My best friend actually locked my precious racing homers out of their loft to be sure the falcon would not go elsewhere!

George lives today because I was not violent in my youth.

To complete my frustration, I did not share in the delight of catching the first falcon—albeit partially trained—we had ever seen. Nor did I see it close up before George found its owner, for I could only justify one day away from school for trapping this representative of the breed of hunting bird allotted to kings during the Middle Ages. Truly my initiation fee into the raptor fraternity was paid with pigeons and with disappointment. I clearly remember reciting a cliché to myself at the time: "If you can't beat 'em, join 'em." I have been hunting for and with hawks ever since, not to recoup my losses but to exult in a natural lifestyle that I do not wish to see vanish from the world my children will inherit.

4

WHY RAPTORS?

Since I had just finished graduate school and was anticipating a second major rearrangement of my life, it was understandable that the Eagle Breaks would affect me as my youthful change of avocation from pigeons to raptors had twelve years before. The flexibility of boyhood must certainly have brought about a peace between my discordant loyalties, as I was not particularly torn by the sudden realignment. But the reasons for the substitution were not fully appreciated until later.

I have been asked many times, "Why are you so attracted to birds of prey?" I used to say, for lack of a better answer, "They just have something extra that gets into your blood." With the Eagle Breaks before me, an understanding began to develop of the obsession that now provides me with endless recreation, more friends than hours allow, and a stimulating and rewarding profession. Time by myself near the Breaks not only yielded freedom to explore but also freedom to think about such questions as "Why raptors?"

I returned to the Eagle Breaks the day after finding the Foundation and Indian Eyries. Only a blizzard or a gully washer would have kept me away. About eight miles south and east of the Foundation Eyrie, I found a pair of eagles repairing a nest in a large cottonwood tree near a dry creek. The Cottonwood Eyrie was twenty-five feet above ground and supported by a large crotch at the center of the well-rounded, solitary tree. Other trees were several hundred yards away, both upstream and downstream.

Finding eagles in the sparse leafless woodlands of the shortgrass prairie is not difficult. Owing to the lack of moisture, nearly all native trees grow near natural springs and creek bottoms. Because of the fitful water supply, usually only a few trees stand on one bank or in the creek bed itself—hardly exemplary of one's idea of a forest, but very suitable nesting places for prairie raptors that normally nest in small groves.

I learned a valuable lesson at the Cottonwood Eyrie: much can be gained by watching nesting raptors from a distant automobile parked where the birds are accustomed to seeing men working. The birds at the Cottonwood Eyrie did not take wing when I stopped near a windmill two hundred yards away. They watched me for several minutes each time I arrived, but even that pause in their normal behaviors shortened as the season progressed. Once I was in plain sight, however, out of my truck, I was a source of alarm: behaviors were repressed, and observation was largely unproductive.

During my visit that day, the tiercel, somewhat blacker than his mate, perched on a limb just above the nest rim until he became habituated to my presence. The female fetched a stick for the nest within a few minutes of my arrival. I reveled in her tacit acceptance of me!

Her repeated actions in leaving the growing structure were monotonously performed: she slowly launched herself off the nest and swerved to miss a branch as she descended about twenty feet; then she glided, very low to the ground, no more than seventy-five feet downstream before spreading her wings to brake for landing. She rarely flew farther down the creek to find nest material, for the bed was littered with dead branches brought by high waters during years past. And she rarely glanced toward the windmill where I sat humbled in my effort to characterize the nature of such a beautiful creature.

The eagle's acceptance of me was the first flicker of response to my difficult question. Birds of prey have qualities that people can identify with, even though the mind's eye cannot formulate the attraction. At fourteen I did not understand the mystique of catching a gyrfalcon red-handed atop one of my best pigeons; the strong-footed bird, wild with strength and fierce aggression, had busied itself plucking feathers from the prey, with me kneeling, talking softly, reaching out, and almost touching it. Since that time, I have been accepted, to a degree, by many wild and captive birds of prey, including the female eagle that continued to build her nest while I watched that March morning.

Oh, I can almost feel the hackles of professionals rising and the disbelief of other doubters as they read these words. Who is to judge a bird of prey's acceptance of man? That is an easier question to answer: simply, any competent falconer, a few contemporary biologists, but no one who has not felt it!

The necessary feeling is derived, in large part, from the astonishing paradox present in raptor behavior. I am amazed every time I think about the mixed conduct of birds of prey; it makes my discordant loyalties look like a choice between two chocolate bars. I shall explain.

In the wild, a falcon will often fly away at the first sight of man— eventually to procure its next meal in a fierce flurry of feathers. Yet if such a bird is trapped, a skilled falconer can train it to his command. Even in the polished companionship of falconry, an aggressive falcon will swoop onto its prey, knock it to the ground, grasp it, and quickly perform the *coup de grâce.* Then, in a master stroke of self-contradiction, the bird will instantaneously return from frenzy and sometimes drag the kill a few feet toward the approaching falconer to accept a tidbit of other meat from his fingers. The same turnabout occurs in the wild each time the male raptor makes a kill, takes it to his incubating mate as an offering preceding nest relief, and then settles himself gently onto their fragile eggs.

Thus the versatility of birds of prey allows considerable latitude for personal involvement with them—just as I rapidly became involved with the eagles at the Cottonwood Eyrie.

Walking in the dry, gravel-strewn creek bed, the female eagle was completely out of her element. Although evolution had supplied her with a rigid pelvic skeleton to support her body when she was walking, her legs did not function with the finesse of her wings. Each beginning step was taken as if she had never walked before. Her slow, high-stepping starts were followed by several rapid, lumbering footfalls toward a definite goal. She moved like a child with newfound two-legged mobility, waddling unsteadily from pillar to post. To me it was undignified and ludicrous, beneath the station of such a masterful flier, but it took her to a piece of gnarled willow root about two feet long and half an inch in diameter. She picked it up in one foot, and with three or four simultaneous clumsy steps and wing flaps she became airborne.

The last part of her approach to the nest was also stereotyped:

always from the same direction, into the wind, and always to the same perch near the nest. Several times, landing with a large stick trailing behind her, she nearly knocked her mate out of the tree. A short hop to the nest was followed by placement of the stick, a painstaking task that often took more than five minutes.

I found it difficult to believe that she was not actually thinking about her actions. She seemed to study the placement of each stick in advance; thoughtfulness was displayed in her posture and movements. But, as others have done for me, I must play down the idea that birds think—at least until more facts are available or the students of animal behavior redefine their terminology. Oh, birds do marvelous and complex things; and learning—through conditioning, primarily—plays a definite role. But instinct, not thought, is the basic process. Birds do not fall in love, mate for life, breed for pleasure, and live happily ever after; there is no passion, no conscious affection, and no fetish for physical beauty.

Rather, there are stereotyped chains of behaviors—fixed patterns of action. Breeding birds "know" when and how to behave properly to bring about breeding, but they do not appreciate that procreation is their goal, just as migrating birds apparently "know" the direction they must travel, but not where they are going. To birds, goals are more immediate, like walking to a stick after seeing it or flying to a particular limb once they are in the air. The chances are that the limb will affect a bird in the same way each time, to produce the same response time after time until some other circumstance, such as egg-laying, alters the instinctive action pattern.

I look back on my formal education as a fixed pattern of action. I was like a bird: possessed by instinctive motivations, made to conform or to be stereotyped, conditioned by rote learning, and not expected to think a great deal as I prepared for test after test over material outlined by someone else. I was a slave to sequences of requirements and to the accomplishment of countless immediate goals; and, as with breeding or migrating birds, there was no guarantee that the long chain would not be broken or that the distant goal would not eventually prove elusive.

Many educators today believe that their occupation requires—of both students and themselves—thinking chiefly, learning secondarily, and instinctive drive only in small part. In my experience, where genius was lacking but persistence was not, both the chronological order in which the three aspects of intellect developed and their degrees of importance were reversed. Because of the awareness of that reversal, I have empathy with my chosen animals. The deep-seated self-restraints of their instinct has led me to meaningful parallels between raptors and myself, if only for my own benefit; I have, in fact, walked perhaps a quarter of their mile, and I say that in peaceful solitude, not presumptuously.

The tiercel at the Cottonwood Eyrie, apparently convinced that my truck posed no threat, tardily joined his mate in gathering sticks. His flight path was virtually the same as hers. As he landed following one sortie, she raised her tail high into the air and stood straight-legged, thereby elevating herself above a normal perching posture. With her body tipped headfirst into the nest, she flitted her tail from side to side, as if mating, and at the same time played with small sticks in the nest cup, as if distracted from the sexual drives that dominated her behavior. She kept her mate in full view by cocking her head. Such female solicitation and sham mating are important courtship behaviors of many raptorial birds.

After nearly an hour of nest building, the female flew off down-stream, leaving her mate perched near the nest on his usual branch. She landed on a prominent knoll in full view of him and began preening. The male also preened, but remained in the nest tree for several minutes before flying to the knoll.

As he flew toward his mate, she assumed the same posture as before: straight-legged, tail up, and head down but turned to watch. He landed on the ground next to her but immediately jumped to her back to mate, his feet balled so as not to injure her, his body balanced by flapping wings and by the full length of both tarsi. Her head-down and nearly horizontal position was important; if she stood normally, with her body slanting posteriorly, her mate would simply slide down her back; with-out her tail raised, his tail would slide across the top of hers instead of locking with it. Theirs is a delicate act, despite their size.

Golden eagles copulate periodically from six weeks before egg-laying to several weeks after. Each time, there follow long bouts of preening and other seemingly vain performances. Each pulled and combed its feathers thoroughly, she atop the knoll and he in a tree gained soon after dismounting. Their privacy was invaded only by cattle preoccupied with their cuds, meadowlarks and horned larks en-grossed in gathering their fare, and me brunching on the usual: a cold sandwich and a soft drink.

When I had finished eating, the eagles were still perched in the same places. I left to begin searching for other nests and more excitement. Three miles west along a well-traveled road was a man-made pond for

watering cattle. Years before, a farmer or rancher had built a small earthen dam across the creek upstream from the Cottonwood Eyrie. A mile farther west, I took a trail north about six miles, across a fairly monotonous stretch of prairie, to Antelope Reservoir.

Two ferruginous hawks were sitting in separate trees not far from a dead cottonwood that held a large stick nest at the north end of the reservoir. I had learned from the experiences of others that these large buteos—or soaring hawks—deserted their nests more readily than other raptors, particularly just before and during incubation. From a distance, I watched them do little more than reflect the sun from their immaculate white breasts. Several minutes later, convinced that they did not have eggs, and not wanting to interfere at a touchy moment, I drove on.

From Antelope Reservoir, the trail ran east a mile before branching south toward the Foundation Eyrie and north into country new to me. I thoroughly enjoy exploring new areas, as most people do, I suppose; so I turned north, passed a trail that veered west, and then came to more monotonous grassland. There must have been two hundred square miles of prairie (but not a suspicion of a nest site) visible at every moment.

OIL WELL EYRIE

I eventually returned to the trail that went west. It coursed along a tree-less creek bottom where torrents of other days had cut a series of high banks into the sides of rolling hills.

On one of the banks, near an oil well, another pair of eagles were building a nest in preparation for laying eggs. I drove on past the eyrie without glassing it, because the road came close enough to analyze the situation completely. Only one eagle was present at the time, and it sat directly above a large stick nest tucked into an irregularity near the top of the bank. It was a "walk-in," a fact I put away in my mind until I actually visited the nest many weeks later. At another fork in the small road, I turned and drove back to a second oil well about a quarter of a mile away from the new eyrie. I hoped that the birds would be accustomed to seeing trucks parked near the wells. My pocket watch said quarter past one.

Most courtship of golden eagles is aerial—spectacular dives, mock battles, and other aerobatics. After I had waited for half an hour, the perched eagle left the bank and climbed to more than two thousand feet, in my best estimate. I had to step out of the truck to watch, but that did not seem to change the bird's behavior. It was soon joined by another eagle, presumably its mate. They soared together, mostly over the eyrie, for several minutes. Finally, one bird positioned itself several hundred feet above and upwind of the other. With wings half folded, and with convincing speed and directness, the higher eagle made a swooping approach to its mate. I assumed, thereafter, that the "attacker" was the male. At the last moment, his mate flipped upside down to present open talons in mock combat, but she quickly regained herself and dived several hundred feet. The tiercel passed over her, leveled his path, then quickly climbed a hundred feet, letting the force of the follow-through from the dive carry him upward. But, seeing his mate growing smaller below him, he immediately folded his wings and dropped toward her again, repeating the previous false show of aggression. I hated to see him surge by her, because that meant the end of another spectacular stoop; nothing plummets quite like a golden eagle. His third approach was a slow, shallow glide, legs extended downward and yawing from side to side. His mate was moving off to the east as he pulled in six feet behind her. Together, in tandem, they turned northeast, away from the Foundation Eyrie and certain territorial conflict. My field notes said only: "Eagle courtship flight!" I will be able to replay that flight in my mind as long as I live.

An hour later, the female returned directly to the nest. I was almost ready to leave, thinking that the birds had merely visited the Oil Well Eyrie but would nest somewhere else. After arranging a few large sticks that apparently looked out of place to her, she settled prone over the nest cup. There she remained for more than half an hour, surveying the surroundings and moving small sticks to their proper places. I changed my mind about the Oil Well Eyrie being an alternative nest site.

Only those bits of nest material within reach of her outstretched neck and beak were moved. She closed her eyes and slept for five minutes or less on several occasions. But mainly she watched: up the creek and down, below the eyrie and in the sky. Apparently, she was evaluating, through instinct, the stimuli coming from the habitat, the nest position, and other features of the nesting situation meaningful only to eagles. Pre-incubation behavior, such as lying in the nest before eggs are deposited, is but one way that instinct prepares each parent-to-be in detail.

There is no time more critical to the success of a nesting attempt. If the nest surroundings present the wrong stimuli that early in the cycle—for example, a man too near the nest—the birds will go elsewhere or will not nest at all. I was locked to my parking place until the situation changed. That known nest site was worth more to me than a half-dozen potential eyries yet to be found.

Eventually, the tiercel flew to his sentinel post, an old nest a hundred yards down the creek on the same bank. He apparently had a more sheltered and less conspicuous place to use during inclement weather, another nest on the opposite bank and closer to my parking spot. His mutes, or excrements, showed below each perch like white flags in a land otherwise void of white, except when certain wildflowers were blooming or when an antelope flashed his shining posterior.

At about four-thirty, the tiercel flew to the nest along a rather circuitous route. From his sentinel post, he rose approximately four hundred feet, with his primary feathers fully spaced. He glided a half-mile upstream, directly over me, and then turned crosswind to slip very quickly nearly three-quarters of a mile northeast. He disappeared momentarily over a hill to the north but soon came back in a steadily descending glide toward the nest. I could imagine birds falling silent and mammals freezing along his path, then resuming their separate ways after he passed.

At the last moment, he swept up to the nest edge from twenty feet below. His mate was reluctant to leave; after a couple of minutes she stood up carefully, walked to the edge of the nest, and launched herself just as she would do again and again during her six weeks of incubation. He left, too, so I took the opportunity to drive on downstream, back toward Antelope Reservoir.

I was able to watch the female as I drove along and around a corner, out of sight of the eyrie. She finally flew behind me, so I stopped to watch. I got out and lay down on the ground, unmindful of the dirt but cognizant of scattered clumps of prickly pear. I propped my head up with my coat and found her in the scope out over a ridge. I knew that I could not let her fly outside the field of vision, because she would probably go so high that I would never relocate her.

I guessed correctly; she slowly spiraled to at least fifteen hundred feet in circles over a mile in diameter, but always enclosing her eyrie. At that height, directly over the nest, she began the undulating or roller-coaster flight display that I had read about many times and anticipated like a holiday meal. Finally, I was able to observe it; I have basked in the satisfaction of doing so ever since.

She folded her wings and then fell a hundred feet before spreading her sails, leveling off, and flapping back up to her original height.

With beautiful cadence of movement she dived more than thirty times.

Then I lost her. Damn! I never did see her again that day. She's just a bird, I thought. Then I realized, No, golden eagles are *not* just birds. Their attributes make understatements of superlatives; criticism of them is a miscarriage of intelligence.

There was freedom and excitement in that aerial courtship; motivation and promise of new life in the eagles building the Cottonwood Eyrie; stability and purpose in the shallow profile presented as I drove past the Foundation and Indian Eyries; beauty and a message of the relevance of eagles to man in the actions I viewed from the Foundation Eyrie blind; skill, strength, and expediency in the killing of the cottontail in the snow-bitten wheat-field furrows; and courage and superiority inherent in Jack's eagle-coyote observation.

We must take care not to pull golden eagles down from their place of command with trite praise. We can praise eagles just by realizing that they need no humanization! To the contrary, perhaps we need "eagle-ization." Motivation, stability, purpose, courage, freedom—such are not virtueless qualities either in the instincts of animals or in the wisdom of man. Yet the attraction of an eagle's unique brand of animal magnetism exceeds even the cumulative pull of their natural and aesthetic assets. There is a single word for such supernormal attractiveness: charisma.

Thus the full answer to my once difficult question is that I am attracted to raptors by charisma derived, in part, from numerous stimulating qualities, both natural and aesthetic. Beyond that, the empathy I have with raptors is in reverence to the behavioral paradox that invests their acceptance of man. The whole question "Why raptors?" is a remarkable blend of animal and human nature.

It is a question that all mankind might profit from answering. I am ever heedful of one of Aesop's fables as set in verse by Edmund Waller, a seventeenth-century poet:

> That eagle's fate and mine are one,
> > Which on the shaft that made him die
> Espied a feather of his own,
> > Wherewith he wont to soar so high.

Will we unthinkingly provide the feathers that guide the arrow of our fate? The assignment of Aesop's fable to philosophy or to prophecy falls to you and me.

5

A YEAR
LATER

I spent two summers studying birds of prey full time near the Eagle Breaks. At the start, in 1971, I knew of fewer than sixty raptor nests from casual meanderings in years past and from information provided by friends. By summer's end, I had notes on over two hundred and twenty-five nest sites.

Each nesting season is begun by great horned owls, the earliest nesters of all prairie birds, often before Christmas of the preceding year. Long before eagles carry the first sticks to renovate their nests on the Breaks—during the longest and frequently the coldest nights of the year— great horned owls lay claim to their share of the available territories, nest sites, and accompanying prey resources. Not until seven and a half months later, in mid-August of the following summer, do the latest nesting raptors, Swainson's hawks, fledge the last of their offspring.

My studies depended heavily on the time spread of nesting schedules of the various raptors. For example, in late March, when golden eagles were just laying eggs, the earliest horned-owl eggs were about to hatch; thus I tried to find all the owl nests as soon as possible. Ferruginous hawks and prairie falcons were searching for nest sites; I merely noted when and where they were seen. Wintering merlins (pigeon hawks) and rough-legged hawks were preparing to migrate toward breeding territories in the north country, while red-tailed hawks, marsh hawks, and kestrels (sparrow hawks) were just beginning to move through on migration; I did not ignore the wintering and migratory species, but I noted only their unusual behaviors and migration peaks. Swainson's hawks were still thousands of miles to the south in late March, winging their way through Central America toward nesting areas in the western United States and Canada; they were equally distant in my thoughts at that season.

In 1972, a year later than most of the events of the preceding chapters of this book, I quickly discovered that the four eagle eyries on or near the Eagle Breaks were again active. Only the Cottonwood Eyrie had been moved to a new position: a tree three hundred yards upstream but still about two hundred yards from my parking place at the windmill.

Thereafter, I spent nearly two weeks observing the behaviors of other raptors. In my efforts to find as many nests as possible the summer before, I had not followed birds, except for eagles, from place to place; nor had I watched from a distance other birds of prey at their nests just to appreciate or analyze their behaviors. I was determined to begin the second season with this pleasure.

The first birds I sought were the ferruginous hawks that had fledged three young from the nest in the cottonwood tree at Antelope Reservoir in 1971. I almost beat the sun to the nest one morning, but I found that a pair of horned owls, not hawks, had moved in. A large slanting limb, stripped of its bark by wind and rain, held the nest. The tree on which the limb grew had risen above the grass after several families of homesteaders had built the reservoir nearly fifty years before. I wondered if they had also planted the first trees at the water's edge, for the nearest native cottonwoods stood seven miles away near the Cottonwood Eyrie. But wind moves seeds as it moves sand and tumbleweeds, and animals carry seeds snarled in their fur. Whether sown by wind or an animal, the tree certainly grew because of man's participation in ecology; his toil built the water's impoundment to provide drink for his cattle—and, inadvertently, for the trees.

The appearance of the owls' nest, in its picturesque setting, was different from that of the eagles' eyries in that the incubating owl was nearly invisible from a distance. With her forward-looking eyes covered by heavy lids, and her ear tufts flattened, she blended sedately into the gray twilight indifference of early morning. She awoke only occasionally for quick analyses of the surroundings: of water lapping against the edge of

IMMATURE RED-TAILED HAWK

MALLARDS

the reservoir, of cattle grazing the gentle upslope of shortgrass prairie to the southeast toward the Foundation Eyrie, and of my truck parked in the distance. She watched and listened. Cattle and the first ducks of springtime posed no danger. Nor did the truck, apparently, because she lapsed back to sleep, her eyes closing halfway, and then completely, as slowly as they had opened.

Her mate was perched against the trunk of a nearby tree—already, at sunrise, in sleepy daytime tranquillity. His outward peace contradicted the reality of his presence by night, when his bold predatory role in nature would animate the countryside with stark silence and speedy dispatch.

As I walked toward the nest, the incubating owl watched me more closely. The most prevalent sounds were from resident birds: crows, starlings, magpies, meadowlarks, horned larks, ring-necked pheasants, and even red-shafted flickers. All chattered and sang their morning chorus from nearby trees and fence posts. Fresh notes were sounded by several migrants and new spring arrivals: robins, mountain bluebirds, and belted kingfishers.

Scores of ducks bobbled near the southeastern edge of Antelope Reservoir where the wind had pushed them that morning. Small waves

tossed drakes and hens up and down like ships in ocean swells. Groups of twenty or more periodically flew or paddled to shallow upstream portions of the reservoir to feed. These groups varied according to species. Dabbling ducks—mallards, pintails, shovelers, American widgeons, gadwalls, and green-winged teals—were forced to skirt the shore to reach food on the muddy bottom by tipping headfirst into shallow water. I missed the teals and gadwalls that morning. Diving ducks—redheads, canvasbacks, lesser scaups, and buffleheads—foraged deeper, even in the greatest depths near the dam. It was nice to have so many divers on the water, although I noted only two pairs of canvasbacks among the many redheads.

Most mallards were already paired. In full spring dress, the green-headed drakes sometimes herded, sometimes led their mates from place to place, as much interested in courting as in feeding. They mingled freely with three great blue herons standing several feet from the eastern shore. Twice, one of the herons leaned forward, took a few stalking steps, and darted its daggerlike bill to catch small carp.

Near the owl nest, the living trees barely showed signs of spring; tiny buds tipped each branch, but six weeks would pass before they opened fully into leaves. Better that, though, than no promise of greening, as on the dead limbs I climbed to get to the nest. The rotten branches were not at all reassuring to a lonely climber miles from town. As I climbed, I made false promises to the owl and consoled her with kind words to get her to leave. She flew off gracefully when I was ten feet below her, but she remained unconvinced—I am sure—of my harmlessness.

Three eggs had been laid during the first week of March, as I determined later by calculating back from the hatching date, using an incubation period of twenty-eight days. Local weather records showed that the last egg had been deposited during a cruel late-winter blizzard followed by three subfreezing nights. Only the parent owls' attentive incubation saved the two eggs that subsequently hatched; perhaps one egg had, in fact, been chilled.

The nest was about two feet in diameter, sloping from the edge into a three-inch-deep cup. Nothing had been done to repair the ravages of winter; the plain white eggs were simply laid on a disordered mixture of small bones and fur—indigestible prey remains regurgitated as tightly packed pellets twelve to eighteen hours after each meal. Many oval-shaped pellets had been casually cast, crushed, and matted into the nest cup. The ground below all the good perches near the nest was also littered with castings, some intact, others broken and disintegrating.

A long record of life supporting other life lay on the ground.

Naturalists use the pellets of fur, feathers, and bones to analyze owl food habits. Upon breaking those pellets apart, I found remains of rabbits, kangaroo rats, gophers, and pheasants. Closer inspection probably would have revealed bones of several types of mice and voles, but not waterfowl, doves, or small birds. Flightless fledgling birds often fall prey to owls, but most birds migrate south in the fall and return as strong and elusive prey, unlikely to show up in owl pellets during late winter.

Nor did I find bones of ground squirrels. The thirteen-lined ground squirrel constitutes about a fifth of the total diet of large raptors near the Eagle Breaks, but few are killed by great horned owls. This ground squirrel hibernates in winter, and it is active only by day during warmer seasons. It escapes horned owls primarily through the timing of its annual and daily behavior patterns.

By exercising their natural prerogative of first come, first served, the owls at Antelope Reservoir forced the builders of their nest, the ferruginous hawks, to use a less desirable territory in 1972. I discovered this later the same day after following a pair of ferruginous hawks I saw perched on utility poles about a mile north of the reservoir. After nearly two hours of perching on adjacent poles, they flew off cross country toward the reservoir, leaving me far behind. I promptly drove to what I suspected was their destination. Above the brink of an intervening hill I saw the hawks circle low over their old nest, now filled with one immense female owl and three eggs. Almost immediately, the evicted hawks retreated toward a different nest site.

They first flew to a small cliff east of the trail near the Foundation Eyrie. The tiercel eagle, airborne as I topped the hill near the eyrie, made a menacing pass by the little bluff and chased the female hawk away. Her mate followed as the eagle returned to his usual cliff-top perch, his message delivered without physical contact.

Generally, golden eagles will not tolerate ferruginous hawks, North America's largest hawks, in their territories, especially as close as a hundred yards. This is an exception to the rule that different species coexist peacefully: competition for food is too keen between these birds. Wherever ferruginous hawks do nest perilously close to golden eagles—or prairie falcons—the hawks are usually intimidated and rear fewer young, perhaps only one or two instead of three to five.

At this point, I lost the hawks for about half an hour, but found them perched two and a half miles west at a nest site I called Honey Locust Shack. The year before, Swainson's hawks had nested here, in a lone honey locust tree near a leveled wooden shack, and had fledged three young.

A few sorties to collect nest material ended the day of nest searching by the ferruginous hawks. As the sun settled on the pink horizon, long evening rays highlighted a placid scene: two hawks perched side by side near the nest, unappreciative of the pageantry of a western sunset, but ever aware of each other. Their pure white breasts reflected the sun's rays. When the male scratched his head, the ferruginous, or iron-colored, feathers of his flanks flashed the same hue as his upper back and the smaller, covert feathers of his wings. In a soar, when his feet are tucked beneath the tail, these dark leg feathers form a **V** between his white breast and tail.

His identically colored mate preened vigorously, arching her head gracefully over her back to reach her tail. Each white feather was tinted with rust increasing in intensity toward its base. Plume after plume snapped back into place upon being released from her large beak tip.

Finally, several minutes apart, each bird "roused" (shook its plumage); the fluffing and shaking loosed several small feathers that drifted downwind on a light breeze. Each raised one foot beneath the cover of its white-and-chestnut-barred belly feathers. The sun had disappeared. Soon, with heads tucked beneath the feathers of their backs, they were sleeping. The silence of the prairie was broken only by the distant yaps of coyotes; crickets and other noisy insects were still in winter dormancy. Even the routs and lows of cattle, many carrying almost full-term calves, ceased for a time. The hours passed unnoticed.

I, too, slept well that night, though I was seventy miles away.

The next morning, daybreak colored a partly cloudy eastern sky like a floral bouquet as I drove back to the Breaks to continue following the ferruginous hawks. A half-hour before sunrise, large cumulus clouds that had passed during the night blossomed like yellow roses in the increasingly golden sky. Ducks trailed across the sky in groups of four or five, silhouetted in the morning's gold on their flight to Antelope Reservoir where the owls were settling into their usual daytime positions. A cock pheasant cackled a sharp announcement of dawn, and several meadowlarks yodeled greetings to the new day from weatherworn fence posts.

The ferruginous hawks also awoke early. The male flew from the tree before his mate, apparently rising to meet the sunrise. At five hundred feet, he still had not reached his goal, and wheeled slowly down to a better hunting altitude. There he held steady in a stiff breeze at a hundred and fifty feet, but soon plunged onto a pocket gopher that was out of its tunnels and foraging above ground.

Northern pocket gophers fall prey to hawks and owls more often than to eagles and falcons. Ferruginous hawks take their share. Many aspects of the life of gophers increase their vulnerability to predation. In late March and early April, as the first horned owls hatch, males are above ground searching for mates. This provides hawks and owls with a much needed early-spring food source. Throughout the year, gophers commonly sit in the entrance of their tunnels without exposing their whole bodies. From there they eat all vegetation within reach, unearthed just enough to be detected by the keen eyes of crepuscular and nocturnal predatory birds. Deficiencies in hearing and eyesight (in comparison with other rodents) expedite the natural demise of gophers in such situations. Later, in midsummer, young gophers forced from their parents' territories commonly fall prey to raptors that are feeding their young.

Safety lies within the tunnel.

The tiercel hawk began eating the gopher, but relinquished it to his mate when she arrived at the kill site. Another hunt brought a second gopher to his grasp. This time he climbed to about a hundred feet and

MEADOWLARK

wheeled in the air currents, his head and eyes cast down always onto a different swath of prairie. I have even seen ferruginous hawks hover momentarily, no small feat for a bird so large. Each consecutive circle overlapped but did not coincide with the previous circuit. His "wing windows" gleamed in the ever more brilliant morning sky. The middle primary feathers of ferruginous hawks are lighter in color than the wing tips and the secondary flight feathers nearer the body. This gives each wing a "windowed" effect that breaks up the typical raptor silhouette—an aid, I suspect, in concealing the hawks from their prey. Concealment is a valuable asset to a predator that must hunt from above and in full view of its prey. The trick apparently worked on the second gopher; its slight movement brought the hawk down to partake of a meal.

The gophers were devoured about three-quarters of a mile apart. Each hawk bolted large pieces of warm flesh into its enormous gape. The prey was held to the ground by the hawk with three forward-placed toes and an opposable hallux, or big toe. Pieces were torn from the prey with the beak by simultaneous raising and twisting of the birds' heads, though most of the upward force came from a powerful straightening of the entire body. Bones splintered and were eaten along with fur and flesh, some of which would be cast up in small pellets—small because hawks digest more bone than do owls.

Near the conclusion of their meals, the heads and hind legs of the prey passed to their crops. Only the prey's intestines were discarded, but even that was not a consistent habit. After feaking—the cleaning of their beaks on the grass—the hawks took wing; both had fed before the sun rose above the horizon. They hastened the sunrise—for them—by soaring up into the direct rays, which struck them at two hundred feet. Within minutes the prairie was awash with sunlight and much of their quarry was no longer available.

The hawks continued to search for a nest site after their gopher breakfast, even though sticks had been added to the old Swainson's hawk nest the previous evening. They visited a nest placed flat on the ground and added several more sticks to the Swainson's hawk nest.

The site finally chosen was, at first, only a haphazardly woven basket-shaped collection of barbed and bailing wire that I had noted the summer before about twelve feet off the ground in a Chinese elm. Such use of wire was a habit of white-necked ravens, a species with a much reduced range since the virtual disappearance of large native herbivores from the Great Plains. The remains of large mammals, such as bison, were an important food of the ravens. The species has now altered its range to include, primarily, the southwestern United States and Mexico, where more animal carcasses and other year-round food can be found. None now nest around the Eagle Breaks, but I did not hesitate, upon discovering the facts, to name the new ferruginous hawk nest Raven Tree. Relics of their wire-nest foundations still remain.

During the next several days, the ferruginous hawks built a platform of sticks that hid the wire base. Branches up to an inch in diameter were used. A second new covering and a nest rim, both consisting of smaller dead roots and branches from bushes and shrubs, were added. Each stick was placed carefully, but not actually woven into the growing structure.

The final touch was lining the cup with small twigs, bark from the dead nest tree, dried grass, and dried cow dung. Large chunks of dung are usually placed on the sides of the cup. This practice—made possible by cattle, man's replacement for bison on the shortgrass prairie—is not as noticeable after the eggs hatch as before.

Ferruginous hawks build nests large enough to hide themselves when incubating. A nest viewed from slightly below and from a distance often appears absolutely empty, although the female is usually there in season, her body flattened onto the nest and eggs. They are equally discreet about where they nest, preferring secluded trees to those close to human activity. Their coy behavior often prevents detection by natural predators and men—including myself.

I did not follow just the nesting species during the early days of the 1972 season, although the days often began—as did March 28th—near the owl nest at Antelope Reservoir. Because the reservoir rarely went dry, it was an excellent source of food for waterfowl and shorebirds. Hundreds of ducks, sandpipers, plovers, and other water birds dotted the rippled surface and muddy edges of the water every late-March evening and the following morning before lift-off on the next leg of long northward journeys. Man had built an excellent restaurant for the birds, and it served them well.

That morning, nature had me observing in several directions even before I left the reservoir. I watched a rough-legged hawk flying slowly along the eastern shore of the water, and then I noticed a dark mass in one of the trees at the head of the water. Why haven't I seen such a large stick nest before? I thought. Adjustment of the scope brought into perfect focus a sleeping porcupine, not a stick nest.

As with the raccoons whose tracks I had noticed earlier near a tree toppled half into the water, I was surprised to find porcupines in the arid shortgrass prairie. How did such mammals live and reproduce in the three hundred acres of moist ground near the reservoir? But, I reasoned, the basic requirements of the raccoon were met: plenty of frogs, toads, and insects to eat; a permanent source of water to wet the food; and several hollow trees for dens. For the porcupine there were ample twigs, buds, and tree bark as food, and many natural dens among the rocks of the Breaks.

As the summer progressed, I learned that porcupines were common. Most kept to creek bottoms with trees, but they were seen wherever trees grew, even in the few remaining junipers and pines that stood on several north-facing rocky scarps not far from the Eagle Breaks. I must have seen every porky in the area at least once, because of their excellent mimicry of stick nests. I admired their disdain for the hurry-up springtime world passing above and below them in ones, twos, dozens, and flocks. And they are such deliberate climbers: each step—whether ascending, descending, or moving forward or backward on a limb—is taken slowly and with painstaking precision. Had I the same expertise, I might not, later that summer, have broken my ankle. Their every movement is a lesson in relaxation.

The rough-legged hawk circled back; or it may have been another. Many passed by the reservoir each day. They breed in the Canadian and Alaskan arctic, but in winter some occupy the land vacated by Swainson's hawks in the fall. The same land provides different niches from season to season: nest trees and cliffs become hunting perches, overhung eyries become nighttime roosts, and some of the same mammal and bird populations serve as prey for both summer and winter species. Nevertheless, the activities of the seasonal replacements are usually well synchronized; they never compete directly with each other in the fall and early winter, and only occasionally do they do so in the spring.

Rough-legs spend the winter preying mostly on small mammals, using their tiny rodent-catching feet to gather their fare. From a stationary hovering position (not unlike the kestrel), they dive onto any small creature that hazards a movement, though they do not commonly kill full-grown winter cottontails or jackrabbits. This they leave to tractor-trailer rigs racing through the night with eighteen or more deadly wheels. Man's highway toll of rabbits and other animals is made less wasteful, in part, by the opportunistic nature of rough-legged hawks. Golden eagles, marsh hawks, and ferruginous hawks also patrol major roads for an easy meal.

The hovering habit of rough-legs—no other buteo does it so often or so effectively—is an adaptation to hunting over treeless tundra. The object is to take advantage of the relative ease of sighting moving prey from a stationary position. The result is a graceful winnowing of wings, like a butterfly flapping delicately into a stiff breeze but making no headway.

Hovering is abandoned, to a certain extent, wherever leafless trees and utility poles afford adequately elevated perches from which to ambush unsuspecting prey. But rough-legs are slow to learn the fine art of perching, having previously sat only on cliffs and on the tundra. Instead of using large branches of trees, they settle into the small limbs of the crown—often with their feet spread and at different levels! Instead of landing on the platform or tail bar of a windmill, as an eagle would do, rough-legs perch on the top of motionless blades. They are dumped off by the slightest gusts, because once they are off center, their weight helps to carry the blades around. Rough-legs also perch on utility wires frequently, rather than on crossbars and tops of the poles. But their tiny feet do not prevent them from teetering; they must catch themselves with opened wings when falling forward and with spread tails when falling backward. Each movement is overdone until the perpetual rocking motion finally ends the perching effort, particularly if gusty winds compound their problems. Rough-legged hawks are graceful in flight but graceless when perched—except on the ground where they cannot fall off.

The rough-leg soon flew off to the northwest where I could not follow, so I drove south to make a quick check of Raven Tree. I crossed two dry washes, then came upon a male marsh hawk coursing alongside the trail in the same direction I was traveling. I slowed down two hundred feet behind it and followed at twelve to fifteen miles an hour.

The food habits, flight patterns, nesting requirements, physical characteristics, and hunting tactics of marsh hawks differ greatly from those of buteos, falcons, and eagles—enough so to warrant the general vernacular name "harrier" for marsh hawks and closely related species that harry the ground in search of prey. This they accomplish with a buoyant, coursing flight, wings held in dihedral position above the axis of the body when gliding. Such flight allows seemingly effortless scrutiny of many miles each day. They yaw from side to side in gusty winds, playing the irregular air currents of broken terrain and different altitudes. When something promising but indefinite is spotted or heard, the hawks spread their wings and let the wind carry them upward and backward into a stall, so that the same ground can be covered more thoroughly a second time. Usually, from less than twenty feet above ground, the hunting flights end abruptly. Skilled gyrations carry the hawks earthward to catch a wide assortment of animals: rodents, small birds, frogs, toads, snakes, and insects.

I followed the marsh hawk for over two and a half miles to an intersection. It made a sweeping left turn to the east and flew along the road leading to the Cottonwood Eyrie. Because of the mixed habitat around that corner—a creek bed, cultivated land, and grazing land—there was considerable heavy cover, including tangles of tumbleweeds hung up on a stand of fourwing saltbush.

Marsh hawks, like owls, are a lot of fluff but little body. At the same time, they are, unlike owls, a lot of bluff but little strength and aggressiveness. I saw the hawk drop from twenty feet and then, instead of disappearing into the tall cover, it flew sharply upward. Something emerged from the weeds to meet it; a feral cat was my first guess. The hawk seemed startled, but it circled back while I put the scope on it. Another stoop brought a large cock pheasant out of the grass—feet first! Fortunately, no contact was made; a pheasant's kick can easily break a raptor's wing or cut it open. The hawk then landed about twenty feet away, but promptly became the defender when confronted with the pheasant's running charge. The timid little predator flew off to the north, out of sight. He undoubtedly had to wait many weeks before satisfying his appetite for pheasant flesh—when newly hatched and helpless pheasant chicks would be scurrying behind their mothers.

Thus marsh hawks are slack-mettled, and foolishness overtakes them at times. Their redeeming ability is flight, particularly during courtship.

I was no great lover of harriers until I saw them sky dancing. Both sexes are masters of the loop-the-loop, often performing a barrel roll at the top of each loop for good measure. Another common maneuver is a barrel roll at the top of each peak of a roller-coaster or undulating display. They appear dark when passing before a cloud, but against blue sky their plumage colors show; grays or browns of their backs alternate through the rolls and gyrations with glistening white wing linings. Anyone would enjoy such flights, I am sure of it.

I watched the ferruginous hawks at Raven Tree for the rest of the morning, but just after noon I was driven out of the back country and onto improved roads by a heavy rain. As March passed, spring began slipping northward along the Rockies and across the plains with ever-increasing speed. Air flow remained mostly west to east, but an additional factor was becoming increasingly important as April and then May neared: warm moist air from the Gulf of Mexico always moved farther north during the spring. Unpleasant, sometimes destructive hailstorms, high winds, and tornadoes are produced when these air masses clash with cold northern air. Summer's stage is set differently each year on the short-grass prairie depending on the moisture content, maximum wind speed, and timing of spring storms.

6

"YOU THINK AND I'LL DRIVE!"

"Look, dammit—you think and I'll drive! And we'll show them how many hawks there really are around here."

At daybreak on April 1st, Jack Stoddart, my longtime friend and fellow falconer, took over the driver's seat for three months. During the first summer, when I was by myself most of the time, I learned much about field study in general. And I developed many ideas for myself, including the hypothesis that two men could do three to five times as much field work as one man. Most problems of my working alone involved the logistics of searching for nests. Thus I asked Jack to work with me from April through June, 1972, and he accepted, in spite of poor pay and long hours. But there was more than money involved; by the end of my second season we were able to look back on the excitement of having catalogued large numbers of nest sites of all sought-after species: golden eagles, 44 nest sites; ferruginous hawks, 66; Swainson's hawks, 125; red-tailed hawks, 12; prairie falcons, 24; and great horned owls, 52. About two-thirds of the nest sites were occupied in 1972. Numbers of two smaller raptors could only be estimated; conservatively, there were two hundred pairs of American kestrels and a hundred pairs of burrowing owls on the study area each summer.

"I already know there's a lot of birds out there, Jake," I said. "I found that out last summer. What we need to know now is exactly how many there are in each of the different nesting habitats."

Jack continued in his typical role of devil's advocate.

"Are you going to stick to all those damned numbers you dreamed up last year—absolute nesting densities, probabilities of this and that, biomasses, and the rest of that garbage?"

Jack does not doubt all of the number juggling that biologists do, but he does search for the relevance of most computations. His technique is to ask leading questions when he has you one-to-one—without colleagues, reports, or books to back you up. He is a good examiner who could embarrass most researchers if he set his mind to it.

"Yes. The 'damned numbers' are here to stay," I said. "You'll change your tune as we go along."

I was reasonably sure he would change, because I knew that his questioning was both constructive and open-minded. Furthermore, I had worked hard to get a few ideas ahead of him.

I felt that if we knew the "address" of every pair of large raptors in at least a thousand square miles, we could draw much wider conclusions than if we studied just the most spectacular species in their preferred habitat. One shortcoming in our knowledge of birds of prey is that too much information deals with only one or two species at a time. Commonly these are the most charismatic species, such as eagles and large falcons. In addition, we often know about these species only in their preferred habitats or, even worse, only along the most accessible cliff lines, the easiest rivers to float, or the edges of forests. This is due more to mobility and visibility problems than to faulty reasoning; no one is to blame. There remains, nevertheless, no way to make accurate estimates of the total number of raptors in an area using just the most easily obtained data—the gravy.

Most researchers recognize the limits of their data; others do not. For example, ten years ago the golden eagle population of North America was estimated to be eight to ten thousand birds. Yet a recent, technically sound census of all habitats in Wyoming has shown that twelve to fourteen thousand eagles, mostly golden, winter in that state alone. We do not know how many golden eagles there really are! The earlier estimate for all of North America may be low by a factor of three or five or ten.

"Look, Jack, if we can't say how many hawks nest in a combination of prime, marginal, and unsuitable habitats, then this study will be just

IMMATURE RED-TAILED HAWK IN FLIGHT

like the rest. That's the only way we can go beyond what everyone else has done."

"Do you still think that we can find all of the raptor nests in two thousand square miles?" Jack asked.

That was our most debated point. It was easy to see that he had not swung to the numbers side of the game, but I had my compromise position already prepared.

"No," I answered, "but we *are* going to find all of them in the western thousand, and when we get bored, we'll go to the eastern thousand to get the gravy."

"Why do we need to do a thousand square miles?" he countered.

"We've got to have an area that includes everything: bluffs, creek bottoms, cultivated land, and unbroken shortgrass prairie."

"Why unbroken grasslands?"

"Because there's no such thing now," I answered. "There are more trees at abandoned homesteads, along abandoned ditches, and near man-made ponds than people realize, and most trees have a hawk nest in them. All grassland is broken now, one way or another."

"Still, a thousand square miles is a lot of ground, Butch," Jack warned.

"Well, if I did four hundred square miles last year, the two of us can do a thousand—cliffs and all. Besides, that's why I wanted *you* out here instead of some booby I'd have to tell what to do all the time."

Jack was right, though. It *was* a lot of ground. My plan would not have worked in forests, because of poor visibility and the difficulty of checking every tree for a nest. Similarly, because of mobility problems, the ideas would have perished—and me along with them!—in a thousand square miles of desert or tundra. One cannot search so much real estate on foot in one summer and also learn something substantial about the birdlife.

But we were on the prairie. Furthermore, ours was a labor of love lasting ten to fourteen hours a day, six or seven days a week. Weather permitting—and sometimes when it did not—research was all we did. Ask our wives! Each day was essential, because our mile-by-mile search for every cliff, tree, creek bank, rock or dirt outcrop, abandoned building, and utility pole was very time-consuming. Fortunately, most raptors nest in or on such natural and man-made elevations—above the rolling grasslands. Large areas can be searched because the eyries or their supporting structures can be seen from the extensive network of roads and trails used by farmers to reach their wheat fields and by ranchers to tend their cattle herds.

"Well, I'm not superhuman, you know—and neither are you," Jack continued. "If you think we're going to do all that and keep up those roadside counts, you're crazy."

In 1971, during the migration periods, I had counted raptors along predetermined routes in three different habitats. Although the counts yielded information on the timing of peak movements of raptors through the prairie, little else resulted. Jack was determined to end that project for the summer.

"What's wrong with the roadside counts?" I asked sarcastically; we had been through the arguments for and against many times before.

Jack gave me his pat answer.

"They're just plain invalid! Too many variables mess you up from week to week: the wind, the cloud cover, the mobility of hawks, the skills of observers. And you'll see more hawks near roads, anyway, because of the telephone poles."

"So what?" I said. "You still get some usable data."

"Okay, Doc, you choose your weather, your roads, your time of day; and I'll choose mine. Five dollars says I'll see twice as many hawks as you in the same number of miles. And you can drive at fifteen miles an hour, and I'll drive thirty."

Calling me "Doc" had but one connotation: you're the Ph.D.; you ought to know better!

"Hey—my eyes aren't *that* bad," I said defensively.

"Oh, yeah? You haven't been watching hawks as much as I have for the last twelve years. Your eyes still haven't got over focusing on a book a foot from your nose. Better yet, Butch, let's just keep track of how many birds each of us spots first today—at a dollar a sighting."

"Hell, we don't have time for that. Let's each just do a job. As *you* said—I'll think and you drive!"

I had to get out of that conversation quickly. I knew that I would have been a poorer man at day's end, at least by a few dollars.

I suppose one could call Jack my assistant, but he already knew what to look for, how to find it, and what to do after finding it. He knew when to climb to a nest and when he should stay away. If he saw something peculiar, he was capable of analyzing the situation. And he knew the ground almost as well as I the first day we went out together. I had spent a lot of time on the grasslands and in the creek bottoms, but Jack knew the cliffs better, except for the Eagle Breaks.

Furthermore, Jack is a good climber, although he is more at home hanging over a cliff on a rope than in a tree. I prefer tree climbing myself, but I did rappel over a few cliffs. Jack usually beat me to the rope. Sometimes I think he was trying to protect my relatively unphysical hulk from its often overdemanding control center.

"What are we going to do about food habits of the birds?" Jack asked at one point.

He seemed to be licking his finger and sticking it into the wind to forecast the research atmosphere for the rest of the season.

"That's the second priority," I answered. "The I.B.P. guys would like to have some idea of how much prey is removed from the prairie by raptors. And, since I.B.P. and the game department are paying the bills this year, I think we should give them a ballpark estimate, at least."

I.B.P. stands for the International Biological Program. Some of the I.B.P. Grassland Biome studies were conducted near the Eagle Breaks, and part of my plan was to use I.B.P. data on prey populations, our data on raptors, and a few pertinent figures from other studies to estimate the percentage of available prey removed by avian predators each year. I had noted in the technical literature that simultaneous studies of raptor numbers, prey numbers, and food preferences of raptors were almost nonexistent. No predator-prey studies had ever been conducted where raptor numbers were known on a large area—an "average" of all habitats—and where prey populations were censused by professional mammal and bird biologists.

In short, we do not know the ecological impact of raptor populations on prey populations, or vice versa. With what frequency and magnitude does the pendulum of nature swing to the predators and back to the prey? Again, the problems have always been logistical: too much work for too few researchers. The cooperation of I.B.P. scientists, a research atmosphere unique in the history of raptor study, lowered that hurdle. Although Jack and I certainly could not answer the question completely, I was determined to get started on it.

But that took a research team working just on raptors. It was soon evident that Jack would be a teammate, not a helper. He did have a better pair of eyes than mine. If I did not think a hawk nested on some low bluff or in a distant tree, he often did and proved me wrong; I did the same to him more than once. We also abandoned the roadside counts, as he suggested, and set to work just finding all the large raptors in a thousand square miles, as I had planned. What he lacked of academia, I had, and what I lacked of field experience, he had. When he ran short of stamina, he made up for it with strength. I was the opposite—more stamina than strength, just as long as I had something to drink and to munch on.

Most of all, it was just enjoyable having someone along who could relate to what I saw. It took me all summer to tell Jack my stories from the preceding year and the first two weeks of the 1972 field work. Nor did I ever hear the end of his earlier, spare-time adventures with birds of prey, including the one about the two eagles chasing coyotes.

Jack's love of raptors rests mostly with large falcons and eagles; it was not surprising, therefore, that with him driving we drifted ever closer to prairie falcon country. I did manage to coax him past two trees that I wanted to check for ferruginous hawks on our way to the Breaks. But it was his first day out, so I just followed his lead.

"See that tree lying over there?" he said, gesturing as we passed an abandoned farmstead at sixty miles an hour. "Ferruginous hawks nested there in '66 and fledged three young. It's not a very good site for them. Too close to the road. Besides, the tree fell down in '67, and that was that."

We have since recognized that many trees introduced in grazing land near the Eagle Breaks are past prime and that their demise is being hastened by cattle that use trees for shade and rubbing posts. In doing so, they destroy grass around the trees; then wind blows the soil away. This exposes the trees' roots and, coupled with abrasion of the bark, kills them. Many former nest trees at abandoned farmsteads have already fallen; a third of those remaining are dead; and most others are not healthy unless ranchers have kept a nearby windmill in operation through the years to water their cattle and provide extra vigor to the trees.

Jack's chatter continued, and I gleaned the useful from the chaff. But there was very little chaff.

As we passed one set of cliffs he announced, "You are now looking at six prairie falcon eyries. I took Jim to all six of them in one day, in 1962, and we banded about twenty young."

I kept suggesting that we head farther east. "That's great, Jack. We'll get back here, but let's hit the Breaks today. We've got a lot to do out there."

Actually, I just wanted to impress him with some of *my* practical experience. He had seen but had never checked the Eagle Breaks, mostly because of the time involved. He had his own pet series of cliffs: the one we had passed en route to the Breaks and another farther east.

"The Foundation Eyrie is there around the corner where that last coulee is," I said, pointing as we stopped a half-mile from the Breaks. "Can you pick out the Breaks Falcon Eyrie?"

I was giving Jack his first unannounced quiz, but it was like testing him with third-grade math. He knows prairie falcons as he knows his ulcer—very intimately.

"There's a tiercel hanging just over the eyrie right now," he said.

"Oh, sure, Jake; and I suppose it's missing the third primary feather of the left wing," I said, laughing.

We were still half a mile away, but he was right on all counts, except that by the time I got the scope on the bird it was racing back and forth along the cliff near the eyrie. The summer before, I'd had to walk directly under the cliff to find the actual nest ledge. I also had trouble telling male from female prairie falcons at a distance; Jack knew them just by their wingbeats. He passed his first quiz with high marks.

Cliff racing, where one bird (more often the male) repeatedly flies at high speed across the cliff face and past the eyrie or its mate, is a common behavior in early April. Sometimes the male dashes along the cliff in front of his solicitous mate. Her calls—"eechup, eechup, eechup"—are as fertile as the facts of life. Other behaviors also serve to cement the pair bonds: cooperative hunting, courtship feeding, mutual preening, prominent perching, and harassment of other raptors.

The actual eyrie was near the top of a sixty-foot cliff overlooking an enormous expanse of shortgrass prairie to the south. The long, two-foot-high entrance showed little whitewash from the previous year's brood below it. It was difficult to find, unless one had, like Jack, studied numerous cliffs. The ledge was three feet wide and littered with rocks that, from time to time, had fallen from the decaying "roof" of the eyrie. I wondered how often such cave-ins smashed eggs and young birds.

In 1971, the falcons had formed a scrape—a smooth nest cup for their eggs—in the widest part of the ledge by pushing with their feet and beaks and slowly turning in circles while lying in the dirt and sand. That was the extent of their nest building, for falcons—like most owls, but unlike golden eagles and most other diurnal birds of prey—do not carry sticks, bones, or grass to their nests. If sand or dirt is not already present on a potential nest ledge, another site is chosen.

Golden eagles and prairie falcons are able to cohabit the Breaks because each occupies a different ecological niche—a different life station. This often permits them to nest only two hundred feet apart with limited conflict. True, prairie falcons often harass golden eagles, but effective blows are rarely struck. Theirs is not a territorial feud.

Territory, by definition, is any area defended by one animal or a

pair against intrusions of others of the *same* species. An analogy could be drawn with the people of one country defending their sovereignty against encroachment by people of neighboring countries. Maintenance of boundaries is a constant duty early in the nesting season—or when a country is newly established. Most territorial encounters merely warn other birds of the consequences of intrusion through behavioral posturing, threat displays, and vocalizations—like arms build-ups, Fourth of July and May Day parades, propaganda, and the rhetoric of international politics. Direct physical combat occurs between birds, but fatal blows are rare. The analogy stops there: men's wars commonly produce great carnage and destruction of national or territorial sovereignty.

Thus, for territorial reasons, the four golden eagle eyries on or near the Eagle Breaks were widely separated. The closest two were the Foundation and the Indian Eyries, about two miles apart, but they nested that closely only because the pairs could hunt in opposite directions without interfering with each other.

As for other raptors, in the ten to sixty square miles of a golden eagle territory there might also be nests of six or eight other kinds of falcons, hawks, and owls: prairie falcons and kestrels; ferruginous, red-tailed, and Swainson's hawks; and great horned, burrowing, short-eared, and barn owls. The lives of birds of prey are inextricably bound into a multi-dimensional ecological mosaic inlaid with niches for each other, mammalian competitors, their prey, and animals only remotely relevant to a predatory existence. Yet two adult pairs of golden eagles never occupy the same breeding territory; neither do two pairs of prairie falcons. A pair each of falcons and eagles? Yes, albeit belligerently in some instances.

As Jack and I drove on north toward the cliff, just before we turned west toward the Foundation Eyrie, Jack spotted the tiercel eagle hunting on soar over the prairie southwest of us. We stopped to watch the bird high in the bright, almost cloudless morning sky. The warming affection of old Sol, then about forty degrees above the horizon, must have warmed the eagle's spirits as much as it had mine; an eagle usually suns its back, if possible, before taking off in the morning.

The eagle circled closer to us, enough to cause the tiercel from the Breaks Falcon Eyrie to rise, but not to attack. Each soared in his own wide circles—the falcon far more laboriously than the eagle—sometimes a mile, sometimes a quarter-mile, apart. A migrating red-tailed hawk then joined the eagle and the falcon in the breeze aloft. Air currents surely must have increased with altitude, because the wind rushing through their wings allowed even the falcon to soar without flapping. The diversity within the order of birds called the Falconiformes, the diurnal or day-active birds of prey, was etched against the blue sky in the underwing colorations and shapes of a falcon, a buteo, and an eagle.

Most red-tailed hawks moved by the Breaks in late March and early April using major north-south creeks and, where they existed, creek-bottom trees as leading lines or tracks for navigation. Some red-tails moved to cliffs near the Eagle Breaks and stopped for the summer, but none nested on the Breaks themselves. With the exception of male eagles escorting a few migrating red-tails across their territories in the spring, very little interaction occurred between those species.

Western red-tailed hawks—their tails are mostly chestnut in the adult plumage—are common during the nesting season in other parts of the prairie. They nest on cliffs, in piñon-juniper forests, and in dense cottonwood stands along large western rivers. I have even found them nesting on steel towers that carry electric transmission lines across treeless expanses of prairie. In the southwestern United States, it is not uncommon to find them nesting on tall saguaro cacti. Nevertheless, in the West most red-tailed hawks nest in the forested foothills and middle slopes of the mountains—the Rockies, Cascades, Sierra Nevadas, and coastal ranges.

Jack and I must have watched the three birds soaring in their own circles for over five minutes. The ratios of body size to total wingspread of the three species were nearly equal, but this relationship was hidden by the wing shapes. The prairie falcon's wings appeared long in relation to his body size because of their narrow pointed shape. His tail was also relatively longer and narrower than the tails of the eagle and the hawk. This was masked, though, because the falcon's tail was spread wide to grab the lift of air currents in the soar. Other underwing characteristics of the falcon included a black patch of feathers near the base of each wing, a barred wing pattern, and a white breast with small dark markings on the belly.

The wings of the red-tail were also barred. In shape, however, they were different from the wings of the falcon. A glance at the eagle and the hawk showed that their wings were nearly identical, except for size. They were wide at the base and in the forearm region, narrowing just slightly near the deeply slotted tips. The eagle and the hawk were soarers, while the falcon's strong points included rapid level flight and high-speed diving chases. All could dive, soar, and fly fast, but each had evolved a specialty through natural selection. Their hunting methods, courtship behaviors, migratory habits, and countless other factors had come to bear—through thousands of years—on their skeletal frames and muscular systems to mold three different masters of flight.

The three birds continued to soar for several minutes with no direct conflict, facing the wind as much as possible to gain altitude without flapping. Jack and I would have appreciated a little cockfight (all were males, apparently), but the prairie falcon returned to a perch a hundred yards east of his eyrie. Perhaps he was no match for the more accomplished soarers, which climbed until they were mere specks in an ocean of blue sky; yet neither Jack nor I had ever seen a prairie falcon have difficulty climbing above an eagle or a hawk in order to attack it. Perhaps the buteo and the eagle never came close enough to the falcon's eyrie to elicit an attack; perhaps our truck intimidated the falcon. The last two reasons, or a combination of them, seemed most plausible.

Finally, the red-tail set his wings in a slightly bent attitude and, using a slow descent for forward momentum, glided off to the northwest. The eagle, Jack, and I followed a short distance. The birds were wafted along unhindered by local terrain, but Jack had to jockey our rig slowly over unaccommodating roads in second gear.

Somewhere, out of our sight, the eagle reversed direction and came back south. Jack spotted it again—his knack was uncanny at times. Still north of its nest, the eagle folded his wings and dived swiftly for several seconds. The angle was steep; agitated air buffeted his feathers severely. At six hundred feet, within full view of the incubating female, he canceled—slowed his descent—and extended his legs like landing gear below an airplane. As his speed decreased nearly to a stall, he quickly reversed his direction. A second, almost vertical stoop brought him to within seventy-five feet of the ground, where he again leveled off. Dangling his legs beneath him, he flew by the eyrie and his mate at a very high speed. Then he slowed abruptly and landed on his sentinel rock, which was just visible to us around the curving cliff face.

Well done, old boy! I thought. If I trapped another red-tail and released it near your eyrie, would you do that again—just one more time?

However, the bird did not receive my whimsical thought waves. Both Jack and I would have delighted in seeing any part of the exhibition a second time; but the eagle soon took flight and unceremoniously disappeared over the hill toward Antelope Reservoir.

7

SETTING
A SUMMER
STAGE

Spring on the western Great Plains is charged with uncertainty. As if in review of past seasons, winter, spring, and summer recur from week to week throughout April. Sometimes warm moist air is wafted softly over the prairie. Humidity soars, and fog shrouds the countryside before vapors, grounded by cool morning temperatures, are released slowly by the sun's warmth. Then the moisture falls anew the same afternoon as spring showers fill the air with the fresh, sweet smells of a clean earth.

The next day, a sordid sky is likely to grumble loudly and spill a cloudburst onto the grasslands. All living things heed the spills and pelts, because survival of spring storms is their audition for a role in the approaching extravaganza of summertime. Delicate and enfeebled plants and animals fall and die. And one can sympathize even with the strong, for the day after a cloudburst, April, the cruelest month, may blanket the countryside and its wildlife with unseasonably cold sheets of sleet or snow, as if to rid the land of all but the best-suited cast of performers. Life must then suffer a quick, slushy thaw when warm moist air and foggy shrouds return.

Weather truly is the director of nature's play, not only each spring but also through the endless course of evolution. Plant and animal populations are restrengthened year after year—indeed, millennium after

77

BURROWING OWL

millennium—by spring storms and other natural forces. Only the strong earn roles on summer's stage; only they may set life in motion toward generations to come.

As measures of spring's progress in the field, some forms of life provide more visible evidence of change than others. Most mammals move about only by night or live underground and are not easily seen. Inspection of four-legged creatures during early April often reveals curiously distended abdomens. But the chance for such inspection is rare, for laden females must be especially private; their left-handed running when they are carrying heavy mother loads of precious new life plays right into the grasp of hawks, eagles, coyotes, and other predators.

Neither are one's expectations met by early-springtime changes in the vegetation near the Eagle Breaks; yet there is promise in the slowly awakening plants. Brown sheaths covering the leaf buds of cottonwoods foretell a greening during May; willows are usually three weeks ahead, in near-summer trim by May 1st. Open but still tiny sagebrush leaves help new shoots of cool-season grasses and other small plants to tint the prairie green; and shrubs, such as broom snakeweed, fourwing saltbush, and rubber rabbitbrush, begin to show color.

But the most obvious early-spring happenings on the shortgrass prairie involve the birdlife. Birds are everywhere when the grass is greening. Perhaps Jack and I were more aware of feathered creatures, but it is not just the diversity of bird types active during April; the birds' affairs are equally varied. Each species is at a different point along its own chain of instinctive behaviors leading to breeding. Some—Lapland longspurs, rough-legged hawks, and merlins—are still on their wintering grounds. Others also have long migrations ahead: most waterfowl, shorebirds, marsh hawks, and kestrels. Many birds that winter to the south but stop to nest near the Breaks arrive in April: cliff swallows, mourning doves, burrowing owls, and Swainson's hawks. Still others lay eggs before the end of the cruelest month; magpies, horned larks, prairie falcons, ferruginous hawks, and mountain plovers are good examples. A few year-round residents—great horned owls and golden eagles—have already hatched eggs by the end of April; in fact, some young horned owls are nearly four weeks old by then. Finally, the latest species to arrive cannot be found near the Breaks at all until the first week of May; these include lark buntings, kingbirds, and brown thrashers.

In spite of the numbers of latecomers, if a naturalist is not afield during April, fully half the field season is missed. The plot of nature's play is better understood if one is continually reminded of the throngs of performers milling around during their auditions, of the trials that each character had to endure, and of the relative calm or turmoil with which the weather set the stage. Especially for students of birds, the rewards of nature's preparation for summer are as great as seeing young birds fledge in July or August.

Of the raptors that normally winter on the shortgrass prairie but nest mostly in Canada and Alaska, merlins are the most spectacular and among the least abundant. Only a dozen might be encountered casually in a year; they usually perch concealed in leafless forests along rivers and creeks, and in windbreaks near prairie farms.

The female merlin is about twice as large as the American kestrel, another small falcon, but only a quarter the weight of a prairie falcon. Its intermediate size and spirited ancestry have bolstered the merlin's courage and agility to levels far in excess of the kestrel's abilities but equal to or greater than the dash of most larger falcons.

The weather was a sunshiny thirty-four degrees when Jack and I left town at seven in the morning on April 5th. Fog hung above every pond and reservoir, and vapors rose from damp pavement that gathered the sun's heat and dried quickly because of its black color. Farmers were already well into their day: each small community bustled with pickup trucks hauling fertilizer, seed, and gasoline toward outlying farms; irrigated land awaited preparation and planting in sugar beets, corn, and onions.

All that was soon behind us as the landscape changed to dry-land wheat farms and cattle country where it was quieter. We began seeing a few raptors: a rough-leg, then a red-tail, and then two more rough-legs.

"Whoa, truck!" Jack shouted, slamming on the brakes just past an abandoned and dilapidated building. "There's a merlin sitting back there."

"Well, stop, dammit," I commanded after he had already slowed down several seconds. "If you'd drive slower, we'd see more things like that."

"Well, what more do you want—I saw it," he said, jerking us into reverse.

The old barn had a definite southeast tilt caused by decades of wind from the northwest. Every time rain or snow fell, it dropped through the roof, which had been nearly stripped of its shingles. Some of the roofing littered the lee of the barn where a farmer had plowed almost to the door to plant every possible square foot.

The merlin held our attention for about half an hour, its feathers fluffed against the cold. It perched on one foot a hundred feet from the barn, atop a dirt clod left between irregular furrows where the plow had changed directions. Nearby, a group of fifty or more horned larks fed busily.

The prey seemed to sense that an idle merlin was no threat. I knew better, and decided we should at least see the little falcon fly away. The bird did not have a cropful of food: it was still early in the day; mealtime had to be near.

"Must be a female, eh, Jake?" I asked while we were waiting.

He agreed, judging mostly from size. If it had been smaller, the dusky brown bird could have been a young male. Curiously, the adult female plumage of many raptors is essentially the same as that of all juveniles; marsh hawks are another good example. Only male merlins molt into a bluish-gray adult plumage.

Finally, the falcon placed her other foot down, bobbed her head toward the barn, and took off in that direction. She flew no more than five feet off the ground at first; the closest horned larks rose and circled out to the northeast. Then she darted abruptly over the building's peak, set her wings, and floated slowly over, as if trying to surprise feeding birds on the other side. There were none, but by then two hundred larks were flying helter-skelter overhead in four or five loose flocks. Each time two flocks came together, the birds merged and continued to climb to stay above the falcon. More larks took flight at an ever-increasing distance from her path as she gathered speed and altitude. After two quarter-mile climbing spirals, the merlin was still below a single mingling flock of more than five hundred larks.

The quarry was anxious, though apparently able to outclimb the falcon at will; but the aggressor had been through the "safety in numbers" routine before. Unexpectedly, she increased her wingbeat and climbed with remarkable speed at an angle of thirty degrees or more directly through the beleaguered flock, making quick grabs with her feet at passing birds. Three times she missed before leveling off. Immediately the larks were concentrating directly over her again. They sensed that her climbing grabs were less effective than her level or diving pursuit.

Twice more the falcon dispersed her fated flock from underneath. On her fourth attempt, she climbed at a steeper angle than before and turned on one particular lark that either did not equal her rate of climb or did not fly far enough away. After a fifty-yard dash followed by a desperate dive, the two birds became one speck in the sky. The falcon spread her wings, steadied herself in uncertain air currents, and gainfully pulled the lark close to her body. She circled sharply once and then drifted slowly southeast and toward the ground. The falcon's audition for a part in summer's play up north was rewarded; the lark's was not.

Jack and I set off on a search for the merlin in endless square miles of wheat fields and prairie.

"Man—that was outstanding!" I said, elated at seeing such a flight. "The peregrines at Creamer's Dairy near Fairbanks used the same tactic on ducks."

"I've seen trained peregrines do it, too," Jack said.

"Up there, the ponds are small and shallow," I continued, "and when a peregrine is in the air nearly every duck rises. You know how ducks swing together in a swarm when a falcon is overhead."

"Yes, just like the horned larks did."

"Right, but you can usually pick out the falcon because it's going so damned fast and across the grain of the flock. A peregrine is really a misfit in a flock of ducks. And that's why we could follow the merlin flight so well."

Just then Jack interrupted to announce, "There's your merlin."

I swear, he could find the proverbial needle in a haystack. A two-foot ring of lark feathers was beginning to disintegrate and spread away from the kill site near the fence post on which the merlin sat, her crop bulging with warm flesh. She watched the wind-tossed feathers occasionally; her calm hid the frantic reality of the chase minutes earlier.

Later that day, I climbed to the Antelope Reservoir horned owl nest. How differently merlins and horned owls must respond to the stimuli that control their annual cycles: the number of hours of light each day, the weather, the availability of food, and other conditions of the moment.

We parked at the usual distant lookout to eat lunch before disturbing the owls. The early morning had chilled us, but the overcoats and sweaters required at that time had been shed as the sun swept west and warmed the prairie to a pleasant seventy-two degrees.

"Ten to one says they're hatched," I said, with a sandwich in one hand and the scope in the other.

"They should be," Jack added. "It's April 5th."

"I had owl eggs in one nest in May last year," I said. "They finally fledged during the third week of June. But these birds already have a couple of pocket gophers stacked on the nest, and the female is watching us pretty damned close."

"Yeah, and the male is perched just to the left of her," Jack noted.

The male owl was less than thirty feet away. Usually he perched against the trunks of trees—to conceal himself—a hundred to two hundred feet from the nest. Most often he sat on horizontal limbs two to three inches in diameter where he could grip his perch rather than sit on it flatfooted.

Thus, although the owls had poker faces, they let us know by their behavior what lay in their nest. We felt it safe to climb because, once they are hatched, owlets and other young raptors are quite hardy, certainly enough so to withstand brief disturbances. However, a visit to any bird nest while chicks are hatching can sentence them to life imprisonment in their shells by altering the temperature and high humidity needed for hatching; and a short life it is then!

When walking to a nest, I always carry the scope so that I can get an eye-to-eye look at the birds just before they fly away. Each pair seems to react differently to human intrusion. The male owl flew off when we were about fifty yards away; then I glassed the nest.

"I get a kick out of how they close their eyes to hide," I said to Jack.

"Yeah, but she's watching you anyway," he said. "She's got one eye open a little bit. If she stared wide-eyed at you, her eyeballs would show up like two yellow lights."

When we were twenty yards from the nest, the female dropped low to the ground and flew heavily to another tree. She approached her perch from about six feet below and then swung up onto the limb in a rather sidewise manner to compensate for the wind.

"You keep an eye on her, Jake," I said. "I don't care to be knocked out of the tree."

Great horned owls do not often strike a man, although when they do it is serious. One does not turn his back on them, because not having eyes staring back at them seems to spur their confidence. Once, the year before, when I glanced away from an owl, she flew between me and the other half of a forked tree trunk. Her flight was "silent"—like a speeding freight train!—as she brushed the side of my head with one wing.

Old memories, the owls' usual baritonal scoldings, and their ominous puffing of feathers always make me cautious—indeed, respectful.

"She won't bother you," Jack said.

"I know, but you just let me know if she comes," I said, reaching the nest and continuing, "There's two young and an addled egg."

The owlets were apparently one and two days old. One could hold its head more nearly erect than the other, but raising their heads was still a clumsy undertaking. Their eyes were mostly closed, and their concern was registered with soft high-pitched chitters when I picked them up. Only their raptorial feet, bulging eyes, and black beaks lent them owl-like characteristics. Their feet were soft, though, not yet cornified, and the major blood vessels could be seen coursing in each toe.

"What's for prey?" Jack hollered.

"Three pocket gophers . . . one leg of a full-grown cottontail . . . and some pheasant feathers," I answered, searching the nest litter. "Everything seems to be great!"

It is difficult to relate the personal satisfaction and the compulsion to protect generated by two tiny pink owlets wriggling beneath sparse coverings of white down just after hatching. I am not a great appreciator of owls, but seeing two of them dwarfed by the hind leg of a cottontail is always a sensational experience. To assure their continued protection, we sprinkled the ground around the base of the tree with naphthalene crystals—flaked mothballs—before leaving. That would confuse the nose of any mammalian predator that might have followed our scent trail to the owlets.

As we reached the truck to continue our day's work, the female owl flew to a small limb just above and about ten feet from her nest. She looked over one shoulder at her unharmed offspring with almost visible relief. I knew that she would soon be brooding them again, because great horned owls are devoted parents. One wonders if forgiving and forgetting are parts of the fabled wisdom attributed to our birds of the night.

During April, the affairs of all other raptors fell somewhere between the wintering of merlins and the hatching of great horned owls. In our search for active nests, Jack and I explored the area east of the Indian Eyrie on April 20th. Two and a half miles from that eyrie, a creek had through the years eroded a gap in the Breaks. Jack and I named the area Battle Gap after learning more about the birds that nested there in 1972.

A pair of ferruginous hawks had found a narrow finger-shaped outcrop of rock overlooking the gap that was ideal for nesting. The huge nest—over two and a half feet deep—stood like a turret on the eastern bluff, well outside the territories of the nearest golden eagles at the Indian and Cottonwood Eyries. There would be no harassment of the hawks by eagles.

As we made our way down to the creek from a trail that passed through the gap, we heard the male ferruginous hawk's plaintive cry lamenting our advance. After coming from a whitewashed perch a quarter-mile upstream, the bird circled above us as we walked and watched, half stumbling now and again on rocks and bushes. Fortunately, rattlesnakes were still in their dens; even in midsummer we were always more fascinated by the sky than we were aware of danger from the ground. Fortunately, neither of us was ever bitten.

Just after we crossed the creek at Battle Gap, still two hundred feet from the cliff, I glassed the ferruginous hawk nest.

"Doesn't seem to be a bird there—but the top layer of nest material is new," I told Jack.

GREAT HORNED OWL

"Check the whitewash to the left," he said.

"It looks fresh, and there are several tufts of down hanging on the nest rim."

"There's got to be a bird incubating," Jack said.

All the field signs were present, but the situation remained a stalemate until I whistled loudly and the female showed herself.

"There she is," I said softly. "Let's get out of here."

The instant the hawk stood up, we each did a casual about-face and sauntered back toward the creek. This apparently restored her confidence, for she did not fly.

As we came to the creek again, a new voice—a rapid, high-pitched "keck-keck-keck"—joined the cries of the male ferruginous hawk.

Jack was already tuned in to the situation and cheering, "Get 'im, get 'im—smack!"

I looked up just as a tiercel prairie falcon whizzed past the hawk, which was upside down, talons extended to his tormentor.

"Did you see that, Doc?" Jack said, nearly knocking me off my feet. "Get down; let's watch."

"Hell, let's get out of here," I said. "That hawk is about to get killed."

"Uh-uh, he'll take care of himself," Jack assured me.

The speedier bird flew south out over the prairie, while the hawk regained his self-possession. The falcon acquired two hundred feet in altitude during his half-mile outrun before wheeling around and making a second approach.

"Watch this!" Jack exclaimed as the falcon turned. "Look at the wingbeat—and follow the falcon, not the hawk."

The prairie falcon came at the hawk along a slightly descending course. His maximum speed was short of that attained during a powered vertical stoop, but it was no less spectacular. At top speed his wings were held close to the body, and each wingbeat was a sharp flick instead of a full flap. His speed probably exceeded a hundred miles an hour; no one knows for sure.

The hawk also sideslipped the falcon's second attack, but flew off upstream as the falcon skyed up a hundred feet and departed to the east, as if inviting us to press our search for another falcon eyrie.

Both ferruginous hawks and prairie falcons have a high preference for ground squirrels as food. Their hatching and nestling periods happen to coincide precisely near the Eagle Breaks. Thus both hawks and falcons need the maximum number of ground squirrels at exactly the same time each summer to feed their young. At such times, one pair of raptors may benefit from excluding competitors from its nesting grounds. This is not territoriality in the strictest sense, because two different species are involved. Ecologists call it competitive exclusion. The feuding at Battle Gap may only have represented the pugnacity of male prairie falcons early in the nesting season, but it is the type of interaction that leads to exclusion.

"Well, Butch," Jack said as we began walking again, "you've just seen a tiercel prairie falcon in a hurry. They're really something at low-angle high-speed chases. I saw a female prairie unzip a jackrabbit like that."

"How'd the bird manage to finish the rabbit off?" I asked.

"She just sat on a fence post until I took care of the rabbit," he said proudly. "It was a prairie I trained about three years ago."

"Sounds like a fisherman's tale to me," I said, though I knew it was not.

The trail did not continue on below the Breaks, so we walked a quarter of a mile down the creek—out onto the flat to keep from disturbing the female ferruginous hawk—before legging it after the falcon. The hawk still stood erect as we disappeared around an intervening cliff.

In the next cul-de-sac in the Breaks, no more than a hundred yards from the hawk nest, whitewash covered the rocks below a deep cavity in the cliff; a female falcon stood in the entrance of the dark hole. Again we retreated to let the birds hatch their eggs in peace, hoping that the hawks would soon learn the limits of the falcon's claim to Battle Gap.

From there we drove toward the Cottonwood Eyrie. I dropped Jack off to walk about four miles of creek bottom downstream to the eyrie, where I was to wait for him while observing the eagles. I told him to take his time and where to look for several hawk and owl nests I had found the year before.

We saw very few golden eagles flying near the Breaks during April. Courtship, nest building, and egg-laying were behind them. Incubation was in progress, a time when males and females filled quite different roles. Females left their eggs only briefly—to exercise, to feed, and to tend to other private matters. Males provided food for the pair, incubating only when their mates were away. When the males were relieved of hunting and nest duties, they sometimes advertised their territorial boundaries by wheeling high in the sky a mile or more from their own eyries, but in line of sight of eagles in adjacent territories.

My watchful hours in the comfort of the truck, parked near the Cottonwood Eyrie windmill, were quiet and pleasant. A silent breeze tossed the tips of the tallest blades of grass; the windmill groaned in apparent agony trying to catch a gust to turn the pump just once. At the nest, two exchanges took place: the male relieved his incubating mate for a total of thirty-five minutes. Neither bird brought prey to the nest, and there was no hesitation about leaving or covering the precious offspring. I concluded that hatching had not occurred; eagles make more fuss over nest relief when hatchlings are in their eyries.

I had learned the year before that incubating golden eagles stay with their eggs tenaciously when men intrude—if the eagles are first habituated to such interference. Knowing that the birds at the Cottonwood Eyrie had watched the comings and goings of men for weeks, if not years, I left the truck about forty-five minutes before I expected Jack and walked along an indirect path to within a hundred feet of the eyrie. There I lay down in full view of the incubating female and stared— fifteen-power spotting scope versus supposedly eight-power eyes—into the great depth of an eagle's personality. It was hopeless for me to duplicate her stillness; fifteen minutes or an hour, no matter, an eagle will lie over its eggs without moving a feather.

There was something hypnotic about lying on the ground gazing into the deep brown of that eagle's eyes; it was almost a spiritual experience. The threat of my presence was reflected in the uneasiness of her expression, a look of challenged superiority looming from the advantage of her high nest. Her golden hackles and neck feathers framed the dark sides of her head in striking contrast.

Why would anyone want to destroy such a majestic creature as a golden eagle? I thought. I daresay that guns would be silenced and poisons never strewn over the land if the misinformed could experience a half-hour face-to-face meeting with an incubating eagle.

Seeing Jack in the distance, I crawled a few feet farther away from the eyrie, rose to my feet, and walked back to the truck.

"Any birds?" I asked the bedraggled hiker.

"Two owl nests, one pair of ferrugs, and a pair of defensive Swainson's hawks with no nest yet," Jack answered.

"It'll be a while for Swainson's hawks," I said; we had seen the first one of the year only a week before. "Jack, have you ever tried walking up to an incubating eagle and just sitting down about a hundred feet away to watch?"

"No," he said. "But I've watched from a distance without them knowing."

"That's not the same," I said. "There's got to be vibrations flowing in both directions. Too bad more people haven't felt them."

Then, as we drove toward the next area to check for nests, I described the precious feelings of my observations of fifteen minutes earlier.

8

IN ONE MISPLACED SECOND

Nighttime on the prairie brings penetrating cold and stinging winds. Though I was clad in my heaviest coat, I was not prepared for the briskness of 5 a.m., when Jack dropped me off near the stone blind overlooking the Foundation Eyrie. He was to be on his own all day, searching for new nests, while I did some more eagle watching.

Without moonlight or starshine from a cloudy sky, the early-morning trek was awkward, if not foolhardy; but I had to be in place before the tiercel became airborne. Except for a flashlight, the equipment I carried did not aid my hike. Half a mile through total darkness, I carried my spotting scope, binoculars, tape recorder, notebook, cushion, and the day's food and drink. As usual, the sustenance, stuffed unhandily into a paper bag, seemed the greater portion of the load.

From the top of the cliff, I could see a hint of light in the east, but not enough to help me navigate. Finally, I got through the last eighty feet—on all fours to the bare rock, dragging my junk along with me— which I terminated in a series of precise body contortions to move silently through the narrow entrance. This was more a labor of love than one might imagine, because there is something crazy about my knees; I was not made to kneel, and grinding pains let me know it that morning. I pulled the paraphernalia in behind me and promptly installed a new canvas door to shut out the breeze. Even as quiet as I was, the female eagle must have heard me above the burr of a cricket chorus.

The history of the blind was not completely known. The rancher said that the quaint structure had been there as long as he could remember. Several bird specialists who studied eagles near the Breaks during the 1930s remembered building a stone blind, but could not recall exactly where it was or what it looked like. Someone else had caulked cracks in the walls with cement no more than two or three years before. I was probably just one in a long line of eagle watchers at the Foundation Eyrie.

Once I was inside, there remained the task of settling into the cramped quarters. First, the spotting scope had to be trained on the eyrie and the excess space in the peephole covered before I dared use the flashlight. Having forgotten to bring something to caulk the space with, I lost my shirt to the project, and as I slowly changed attire in the small hut I suffered an attack of the shivers. In total darkness I hoped for fair weather: the roof was unpatched, and I was cold!

The female eagle was lying close over her eggs, idly watching the countryside as dawn came. She intermittently stole short spells of sleep. Meanwhile my teeth chattered incessantly, I exercised my toes and fingers, and my sensitive back complained from end to end. What a tomb, I thought, though the punishment bowed low to the privilege.

About a quarter to six, in cloud-subdued twilight, a coyote moved toward her pups in the nearby den. That, too, was a privileged observation. I had heard howls in the distance from time to time, so I knew that coyotes were about. But seeing one emerge quietly and furtively from the daybreak was new to me. She was light of foot, and she carried her tail lower and ears more nearly erect than any dog of comparable build. It was refreshing to see one walking instead of running away. Yes, I would have liked to know her better, but I had to let the opportunity pass. Undoubtedly, at least four pups, born two or three weeks earlier, whined a welcome to her as they searched anxiously for her nipples several minutes later.

The first cliff swallows had returned about two days before; as the eastern sky brightened, they began assessing winter's damage to their future homes by repeatedly landing and standing precariously on the broken floors and roofs of the previous year's nests. I also heard the male house sparrow chirping his good morning from somewhere on the cliff, and the tiercel eagle flew by about half past seven. His mate and I simply watched him disappear again along the cliff face. That must have been when I stopped shivering; my back had numbed sufficiently, and I final-

ly began enjoying myself. The female eagle and I were there alone, and that was sufficient reward for the moment.

The highlight of the early-morning hours, outside of my appreciation of the eagle, was the birth of a calf directly within the sodded confines of the old foundation. Just five of thirty cows in the pasture were then without newborn. Until long after sunrise, the youngest lay where it had been forced onto the prairie, hind legs folded underneath, head resting between splayed front legs. Its mother stood guard nearby, properly unconcerned with any danger presented her calf by the eagle. There was no threat; the eagle probably had never tried to kill a calf of any size. Nearly all large-hoofed mammals are beyond the size range of prey taken by golden eagles, except in extreme winter and early-spring crises. Then calves are either unborn or approaching the yearling stage—in any case, unavailable to eagles as prey. If pronghorn antelope or domestic sheep are killed by an eagle (a few authentic records do exist), it is by a small number of desperately hungry birds.

At about eight o'clock, the female eagle noticed wisps of dust rising over the hill to the north. Through a peephole in the canvas door I saw the rancher's blue pickup truck crest the intervening high spot of ground and proceed noisily toward the gate. In response to the intrusion, the eagle huddled deeper into her nest, spreading her wings slightly in order to lower her posture more than usual. She extended her neck and laid her head comfortably between two sticks, thereby emptying the nest to unaided eyes below her.

The truck stopped short of the gate, and junior leaped out to open it—no small task for a young boy. He cleared the way by throwing several tumbleweeds over the fence into the next pasture, and then struggled for several seconds—as I have many times—to remove a loop of wire holding the top of the movable post to the firm post. The wires of the gate finally fell limp, allowing him to lift the post from the bottom loop of wire and drag it out of the way. The truck whisked more tumbleweeds through the gate, stirring up a cloud of dust in the process. The boy then threaded the gate behind the remaining weeds and pulled it taut for replacement. Nearly all the weeds had been moved to the downwind side of the fence, free to travel the next mile of their fence-to-fence journey with favorable winds.

The truck soon disappeared from the eagle's line of sight. She dared not raise her head to improve her surveillance lest the movement be detected. My observation point let me watch most of the rancher's progress, but only sounds came to her aid. She had surely suffered that listening routine many times before: every other day or so with the blue truck, and countless times with other vehicles.

Scrapes and rebounds of tires on the bumpy, rutted trail proceeded along a path familiar to her. The steady determined purr of the engine working in second gear dominated the incoming sounds. Then the engine revved, tools in the truck bed clanked, and deadwood from saltbush began crackling beneath the advance of the four tires. She could not see the truck leave the trail and move toward the newborn calf, but she remained motionless, apparently determined not to flee. The truck came menacingly closer and stopped. Tires quieted. Engine sounds ceased. Only mama cow could flee; she scuffled heavily away from her calf and mooed concern from several yards.

A husky voice echoing against the cliff told me of the calf's good health, although the man did not know I was eavesdropping. I wanted to yell at them, but that would have added to the eagle's problem.

The boy's attention was drawn by the swallows' exquisite chatterings, and he noticed the eagle nest. He picked a rock from the arsenal provided by the broken foundation and threw it smacking against the cliff several yards to one side and ten feet below the eagle nest, just missing a cluster of swallow nests. The eagle flinched but sat tight; I did the same with great difficulty. The boy's father, anxious to check the remainder of his herd, cut short his son's threat to the eagle's safety.

"Come on, son. We ain't got time to fool around."

"What kind of a nest is that?" the boy asked, in no great hurry to yield to his father's prodding.

"An eagle."

"Why don't we get rid of it?"

"No reason to," the rancher said. "We've never lost any calves to them, and they eat a lot of rabbits. And what do you suppose rabbits eat?"

"Grass?" the boy answered, not quite certain of his response.

"Right. And what do cows eat?"

"Grass!"

"Right; so why kill eagles?" the man said, finishing his somewhat circular line of questioning.

The youngster paused before changing the subject, apparently convinced by his father's wisdom. "Do you think there's one there now?" he asked.

My heart nearly sank through the stone floor of the blind; then the conversation took a turn for the better.

"I don't know. I suppose so. Come on, let's go," the man said in haste. "Nothing more we can do here."

Doors slammed, and the engine started. After reaching the trail again, the noisy truck silenced in the distance and returned to the eagle's sight over the nest rim. She straightened up in relaxation of her concealing posture as I caught a glimpse of the tiercel high overhead, almost out of sight. Perhaps he had given her moral support—positive reinforcement—during her trial. I was somehow comforted by seeing him lording over us; he wheeled above the truck for over a mile, probably until the far gate was closed.

Relieved of the false threat of the rancher and his son, the female eagle at the Foundation Eyrie began preening. She stretched her neck and cast her head and eyes downward, like a man trying to see his own chin; that was the only way to reach feathers high on her breast. She was a fidgety incubator during the day, frequently in motion tucking the eggs underneath herself, scanning the landscape from side to side, rearranging sticks in the nest rim, and preening. Other incubating eagles are not so animated; they sit stoically quiet as if martyred by their natural responsibilities. Once, she stood up, walked to the nest edge, and stretched her right leg and wing out to her side and downward, apparently to relax the stiffness from sitting motionless. Oh, how I would have relished doing the same; I was tingling from the waist down, but still gloating over every moment.

While the eagle stood away from her eggs—there were two, as the year before—I was able to see a small hole in one of them; it was pipped, just as I had hoped, but it would not hatch for another twenty-four hours, at least. Knowing that, I was better able to understand the female eagle's steadfast endurance of the rancher and his son so close to her nest. She probably had been able to detect the first faint peeps and movements of the embryos at least seventy-two hours before hatching— sometime during the day on April 27th. This heightened her interest in the long ordeal of incubation. As nearly all birds of prey would do in similar circumstances, she instinctively retreated into the nest cup and resisted fleeing, thus helping to assure a good hatch. Females somehow "know" that they must stay with their nearly hatched charges, even when disturbed; this is often not so early in incubation when, at the slightest intrusion, they usually flee their nests—sometimes to total abandonment.

After the tiercel escorted the intruders out of his territory, he returned to his sentinel rock. A few minutes past nine, he flew to the ground near a dead yucca plant not far from the nest. He jerked up on the small plant's taproot by grasping it in both feet and springing into the air—unsuccessfully once, but with power beyond necessity the second time. This he did—who knows why—before most trips to take his turn over the eggs.

I knew about the curious and widespread practice of raptors adding new material to nests during incubation and after, but seeing it firsthand set me to thinking again. Is it a continuation of nest building? Repair? Maintenance? Are the reasons aesthetic or practical?

Some believe that the use of green material results from an artistic sense for ornamentation, though visual appreciation of such artistry by

birds, if it exists at all, is probably of too little importance to be incorporated into a bird's behavior through natural selection. Perhaps there are functional reasons, such as sanitation, reduction of damage to eggs and nestlings, humidification of air in the nest, and aeration of the nest itself. But the quantity of material brought after eggs are laid is small, particularly late in the nestling period when sanitation is most needed. It has also been suggested that because birds remain under the control of reproductive hormones for several weeks after egg-laying, some courtship drives linger well past their peaks. This would partially explain why the addition of fresh nest material decreases as the nesting season progresses; apparently, levels of certain hormones also decrease progressively. Thus the curious practice is probably just a carry-over from nest building that may now be ritualized in the nest-exchange behavior of some species.

The female eagle watched her mate closely as he pulled up the dead yucca plant and flew with it toward the eyrie. Nighttime winds had subsided; he labored in the morning calm, but navigated honestly a straight incoming climb in the feet-up position, the yucca held beneath his tail. He lit on the nest rim and stood for several seconds with the plant clutched in one foot. His head was slung lower than his shoulders as if he were leaning slightly forward, an inquisitive posture in anticipation of his mate's arising. This did not ensue. He released the yucca and shuffled closer, but she just reached out to him and softly snipped hackles on his neck, her head cocked in a sporting manner. Then she retracted her head quickly to look at him from as far away as possible without standing up. He lowered his head toward her but did not reciprocate the snip. At that moment she rose, hobbled by limply closed feet, and stepped backward, delicately opening each foot in turn and placing it on the nest rim. Three careful steps brought her to the nest edge whence she surrendered her responsibility by disappearing below the top of the cliff almost immediately. She reappeared on a prominent point beyond the tiercel's sentinel post where he had cached a dead rabbit—something I somehow missed, unless it had been left the night before. She ate her fill.

The finesse and tenderness displayed by the most powerful of North American birds when it is in a nest with eggs or small young is entirely out of keeping with its predatory role in nature. Golden eagles are as two-faced as spring weather on the prairie: warm, calm, and apparently supportive of life at one moment, but cold, aggressive, and destructive

GOLDEN EAGLE FOOT

an hour later, with talons squeezing life from a rabbit, a pheasant, or a weasel. Such is the great paradox that attracts me to raptors. They must control their aggression, turn it on and off, because in one misplaced second an eagle could destroy its eggs or young. Their apparent devotion as parents is opposite but equal in magnitude to their predatory drives.

As the day progressed, the two large embryos made increasingly more noise. If they were uncovered—and if an observer knew what to listen for—their sounds just carried the seventy feet to the blind. Peep generated peep in an innate mutually stimulating vocal exchange between siblings. This noticeably excited the parent eagles—and me as well! In addition, the sounds probably tamed the adults' aggressive tendencies to kill anything that moved within the size range of their prey.

When he was able to coax his mate to leave, the tiercel reacted to the noisy eggs by cocking his head to listen. Upon returning, the female usually took her position for incubation slowly, preferring, instead, to stare momentarily at the eggs between her feet before muffling the exchange of peeps by settling herself onto the eggs. This she did with several deliberate teetering movements of her whole body—belly feathers fully opened—followed by a few sidewise adjustments of her position. Tiny flicks of her wings insured their most comfortable fold across her back, much as one might shrug one's shoulders to relax in a chair.

Originally, most of an egg is filled with liquid. An embryo cannot peep even if it is well developed, because vocalizations require air. But there is an air pocket at an egg's large end that expands throughout incubation to as much as a fifth of the total volume of the egg. The chick and its waste products occupy a progressively smaller and smaller portion of the egg until, as one of its first tasks, the chick breaks into the air pocket. This allows more freedom of movement, filling of the lungs with air, and sound production.

The pip first appears as a fine cross formed by two intersecting cracks, each no more than a quarter-inch long. After pipping, the shell's outward appearance may remain the same for thirty hours or more as the chick breathes more and more air and becomes progressively less dependent on oxygen exchanged through the shell and its membranes. Eventually more hairline cracks spread away from the original pip, and the chick begins dislodging small bits of shell, particularly near its mouth, as it works in a doubled-up fetal position. Finally, a half-inch hole is formed and the crack begins spreading around the large diameter of the shell.

The first egg to hatch at the Foundation Eyrie was still at that stage when I left the blind for the night—after almost fourteen hours entombed in my stone hut. Some of my leg muscles did not function properly owing to the long period of inactivity, and my equilibrium was not at its best as I crawled out of the eagle's sight and plodded off to meet Jack north of the Foundation Eyrie at the usual parking place. Thoughts of a bath and preening, my wife and the mother eagle, kids and eaglets, and good music and bird songs whirled in my mind. I would have slept the seventy miles home, but I craved a hot meal and the conversation was endless.

"How did you do, Jake?" I asked.

"Well, I did a hell of a lot of walking, since I didn't have anybody to pick me up," Jack answered, obviously soured on having to walk both away from and back to the truck.

"Now you know what I was up against all last year," I said.

"Yes, but it was worth it," he continued. "There's another pair of prairies less than a mile west of the pair at Battle Gap."

"Did you check your eagle eyries out east?" I asked.

There is another series of eagle nests on a ten-mile-long cliff line beginning about five miles east of Battle Gap. Jack had visited the nests on the East Bluffs, as we call them, almost every nesting season since 1961. Everything the Eagle Breaks are to me, the East Bluffs are to Jack. I knew that, being so close, he could not resist a quick pass through his area.

He smiled at being confronted directly and said, "Yeah—the four easiest ones. The Pothole, Great Wall, and Shotgun Shell are all active, but the Cove Eyrie isn't."

"How many prairie falcons did you see at the East Bluffs?" I asked.

"Just one near the Pothole Eyrie," he answered. "He's probably from that phantom pair that I've never found a nest site for."

During all his explorations of the East Bluffs, Jack has found only one prairie eyrie in addition to the mystery pair. Yet the cliff line is longer, taller, and more spectacular, in some ways, than the Eagle Breaks. He had pointed out to me two years before, when we were out for a day, that all the ledges on the East Bluffs are upside down. Erosion of those particular cliffs creates overhangs but not ledges or cavities; yet the surrounding terrain, vegetation, and animal life are the same as those near the Eagle Breaks. There should be more prairie falcons nesting on the East Bluffs.

"How come the eagles do so well on the East Bluffs if there are no small ledges for prairies?" I asked. "It seems to me that there'd be more smaller nest sites."

"Maybe," he answered, "but look at the eyries. The Pothole Eyrie is a natural for eagles, and because eagles nest earlier, prairies never have a chance there. The Great Wall is on a small pinnacle just over the edge of the cliff, and Shotgun Shell and Cove are also exposed."

Jack went on to note that eagles make their own way a little by building nests. Prairie falcons need everything provided: an overhang to get under or a cavity to get into and someplace to make a scrape.

"We could really prove a point by digging cavities into those cliffs," I said, renewing a longstanding idea of Jack's.

Since Jack began studying the East Bluffs, he has dreamed of putting nest ledges for a dozen pairs of prairies on the cliffs with a pick and shovel—or a little dynamite.

"Yeah, but people with money have to wake up to raptor management first," he said. "You can't do it in a day or for a dollar ninety-eight any more than you can manage a population of deer or pheasants for hunters."

I could hear the lament in his voice.

"How'd the blind work out?" he asked, bringing us back to the present activities. There was no sense poring over the management issue on such a good day.

"Wow—I had a ball after I got everything set up," I said. "It even gets warm in there after a while. I discovered that coyotes aren't always running; one walked almost directly under the eyrie just at daybreak. Except for the female fidgeting over the eggs, there isn't an awful lot of action when the tiercel's not around; and he isn't around much. But it's fascinating anyway. They don't suspect a thing! The female seems so self-satisfied and the tiercel so doting when they're both there."

Jack could hardly shut me up once I began talking about my day.

"What about the eggs?" he asked. "Are they hatching?"

"Yes," I said. "I knew we had to get a head start this year because of the warm weather. We've got to be back before sunrise tomorrow, because I think one might hatch in the morning. You can spend the night at my place or else take the day off."

Jack had another sixty miles to drive home beyond my house; he lost a lot of sleep that summer.

"Something I did learn," I babbled on, "was how eagles react to people near their nest."

I told him of the sunrise, the rancher and his son, the nest exchange, and how the parent eagles reacted to the hatching eggs.

When I finished, he asked, "Why don't you let me go to the blind tomorrow? You can go look for other nests."

He knew that he had missed something, and that was hard for him, because no one craves being near the action more than Jack.

"Besides, I'd like to get some pictures," he added, trying to shame me into his plan.

I must have been thinking about my stiff muscles and the hour of shivering that morning when I said, "Okay, but not for the whole day. I'll check those pines west of Antelope Reservoir and be waiting for you at the drop-off point about two o'clock."

It was set; Jack slept at my house. For once, we had actually planned a day's activities in advance.

9

THREE OUNCES
OF SMALLISH
MIGHT

In the shallowest water and along the banks of Antelope Reservoir, many shorebirds scurried to restore the energy used during the lap of migration they had just completed.

Damn—how did Jack ever talk me into letting him go to the blind today? I thought, noting long morning shadows cast on the water by several lesser yellowlegs and countless small sandpipers.

The birds were all gleaning bits of aquatic life from the mud within four feet either side of the water's edge. Recently arrived spotted sandpipers teetered unsteadily on rocks and on the muddy shores: they piped—"peet, pee-weet-weet-weet"—the full width of the reservoir. Frequently, their calls were blotted out by the loud plaints of killdeers—and more of my own muttering about my decision to let Jack watch the eagles.

He'd better make good use of the tape recorder, I thought, spotting a group of American avocets.

I had outfitted Jack with a tape machine because I knew he would talk to a microphone more than he would write in a notebook. I am better at talking when in the field, too; a field notebook is forever in arrears because it demands written composition, a time-consuming process when minutes are precious.

American avocets are the most attractive shorebirds of the shortgrass prairie. Several of these pigeon-sized beauties had also just returned for the summer. Their inimitable bloom included striking contrasts of color: bluish legs, black-and-white wings and back, and cinnamon-colored shoulders, neck and head, plus a long black upturned bill. When idle, they stood erect, delicately balanced on one of their stilt-like legs. So high were their heads above the water that they had to lean forward to gather food; concentric waves rippled away at each step.

Seeing the male eagle from the Foundation Eyrie did not quiet my regret. He left a rabbit kill two hundred yards beyond the reservoir and flew directly toward his eyrie—and Jack! The rabbit must have been caught the day before, because that tiercel was usually a late riser. More

AMERICAN AVOCET

often he waited until nine or ten o'clock before riding thermals aloft in search of food.

Leftovers are a different matter—an easy breakfast, I thought. Besides, he's probably got a new eaglet back at the eyrie.

It was difficult for me to forget about Jack and his privileged point of view. The male owl at the reservoir, asleep in a tree near his mate and two youngsters, finally set my mind at ease. He seemed so tranquil. I could have slept some myself; Jack and I were on the road at quarter past four that morning, after talking about our previous day until midnight.

When I climbed to the owl nest a few minutes later, the parent owls reacted in the usual way: hooting, popping their beaks, and flying from tree to tree. Even the owlets—at three and a half weeks old—grabbed at me with their needle-sharp claws; but I never tired of their abuse. We had dozens of horned owl nests on the study area, but there was anticipation of discovery each time we climbed to one. As prey, would there be two kangaroo rats and a cottontail and three pocket gophers, or a mourning dove and a pheasant head and a grasshopper mouse? Would the parents move off or turn to attack? Would we find two owlets and an addled egg, or three owlets, or one youngster and wonder why not three, or none where we knew there had been three eggs? Our moods fluctuated according to what we found.

Through their boisterous behavior, the adult owls brought a pair of Swainson's hawks down on themselves, the first I had seen at Antelope Reservoir. The struggle between Swainson's hawks and horned owls for control of small groves of trees is probably the most common raptor-raptor feud on the shortgrass prairie, though nesting prairie falcons do not tolerate owls in the air during the day.

The Swainson's hawks blitzed every time the owls changed perches; unlike the evicted ferruginous hawks, the new arrivals left little doubt that they, too, were going to nest near the reservoir. But first they had to put the owls in their proper place or face an entire breeding season in fear of being haplessly snatched from a limb or out of their nest by a very capable—and probably so inclined—great horned owl. Swainson's hawks are always the aggressors in daytime battles; one wonders if the tables are turned at night!

I left quickly to spare the owls more harassment. Two miles south, five miles west, and several gates from the reservoir, I came to the limber pines, ponderosa pines, and Rocky Mountain junipers that I told Jack I would check for nests. Several hundred trees were scattered picturesquely on the sides of a few small canyons and hollows among a series of bluffs too low for most eagles and prairie falcons to nest on.

Such forests are living long past their heyday, the colder and wetter periods of the ice age. In fact, there are no other limber pines between the Eagle Breaks and the Rocky Mountains. Some believe that much of the western Great Plains was sparsely forested until approximately fifteen hundred years ago. As the climate became increasingly arid and wildfires swept the prairie, small islands of trees were left among the unsodded rocky scarps and breaks in the prairie—where fire could not spread.

The first group of pines stood at the end of a half-mile upslope of shortgrass prairie that I could have driven across, but driving was not my way. Jack would attest to the time we spent walking to save the grass. It was not wasted time, though; like sitting in a blind, hiking is a respite for thought and a chance to get to know nature better. Ecology goes by the window of a pickup truck too quickly to suit me.

Whenever I strike out for a cliff line, I always try to walk up a draw or a small stream bed; there, in the sparse cover provided by fourwing saltbush and other taller plants, much of the wildlife of the prairie lives. No more than fifty steps on my way to the pines, a cottontail scurried from underneath a bush to the nearest burrow and disappeared. About me were signs of many more cottontails and jackrabbits. Bushes held tufts of fur where the rabbits were shedding their heavy winter coats. Droppings littered the ground.

Desert cottontails, the true rabbits found most often near the Eagle Breaks, do not burrow for themselves; rather, they find shelter from predators in abandoned holes dug by other animals. Active or recently abandoned prairie dog towns are prime habitat for desert cottontails. Like the horned owl and the hawk, the daily activities of cottontails and prairie dogs do not coincide. Rabbits are night animals; prairie dogs usually disappear underground before the sun sets.

Less than another hundred yards toward the pines, I pushed up another rabbit, a tiny bunny barely three weeks old. Cottontail does are already carrying their second litters in late April, well on their way to producing as many as twenty young before summer's end. Cottontails also breed early in life, and have large litters of up to six young. A high reproductive rate is their method of offsetting high vulnerability to predation. Twenty-eight percent of all prey I recorded for golden eagles, ferruginous hawks, Swainson's hawks, and great horned owls were cottontails—a heavy toll on one prey species.

As I walked on up the slope, two black-billed magpies led me slightly off course to a raptor kill. Probably an immature golden eagle had struck, for I was not in the territory of any nesting eagles. The vegetation changed quickly once I was out of the saltbush; within a hundred feet of the draw the grass was all short, and the sod was continuous— excellent white-tailed jackrabbit country. Did the eagle spot a white-tail in its hiding place? Or did it happen upon a black-tailed jackrabbit too far from the cover of the saltbush?

The magpies held their ground until I was about fifty feet from them, and then screeched their disgust in flight uphill to the nearest trees. Bits of fur from the kill had drifted as much as twenty feet downwind from the remaining bones: both hind feet, a nearly devoured skull, and one front foot—rather slim pickings for the magpies. The feet were definitely jackrabbit, not cottontail; I knew from the length of the leg bones. But only the tail fluff would show me which of the hares it was: white-tailed or black-tailed.

Golden eagles often pluck or strip much of the fur from a rabbit before they eat it, just as they would feathers from a bird. In the process, the tail fur is sometimes stripped, in one fluffy ball, from its bones and tendons. I found the black tail impaled in prickly pear nearby. The rabbit *had* been trapped away from the saltbush.

Although black-tailed and white-tailed jackrabbits often occur together in open country, black-tails are more numerous in taller vegetation, especially grain fields and saltbush stands. White-tails, on the other hand, prefer areas where visibility is best.

Accordingly, the two species use different tactics in escaping predators. Of utmost importance is early detection of danger and then outdistancing it. The favored tactic of black-tails is to sneak off or to run away at the first sign of a threat, usually upwind or uphill to put the pursuer at a disadvantage. White-tails make greater use of their keen eyes; they sit up on their haunches—kangaroo style—with erect ears, sniffing the air, and stretching their necks to better follow a predator. They use all their senses! If they are not hard pressed, they hop away at a leisurely but steady pace, stopping periodically for other upright surveys of the potential danger.

Both black-tails and white-tails, if actually threatened by a coyote or a raptor, lower their ears and bound at great speed across the prairie. Their four feet hit the ground in rapid succession; then a spring into the air carries them three or four yards before they touch ground again. Jackrabbits, if overtaken by a hawk, will sometimes jump high into the air at the last moment and actually let a hawk pass almost underneath. Upon landing, they usually run in a different direction and travel a hundred feet or more while the hawk reorganizes its pursuit.

Hares have keen eyesight, huge ears to collect sound waves, and long powerful legs adapted for extended periods of swift running—more so than cottontails. But there are many other differences between hares and true rabbits. Rabbits are short-haired (or naked) and blind at birth. Younger ones require considerable care from does, which return to underground nests to nurse their offspring. Hares usually give birth above ground in small depressions, called "forms," dug by the adults; furthermore, their young have well-developed fur, open eyes, and move about minutes after birth.

I renewed memories of many nature lessons that morning, but I found no active raptor nests. My five finds included two sleeping porcupines, two very old nests in juniper trees, and another stick nest on a low bluff. This was disappointing, as it had been the year before, because similar woodlands are prime nesting habitat of ferruginous hawks in Utah and Idaho. Near the Eagle Breaks, apparently, there is too little of this habitat to attract nesting hawks consistently.

As I approached one prominent bluff among the trees, seven mule deer bounded across a small coulee ahead of me; far below, a half-dozen pronghorn antelope roamed in the privacy of their own world. I chose a spot near a sleeping porcupine to eat lunch. Stopping was a rare luxury when I was in the field; more often I just grabbed a bologna sandwich and a can of soda pop and drove or walked on. But I had time to spare waiting for Jack, so I relaxed a little. My only real care was whether or not the eaglet in the Foundation Eyrie had made it out of its shell.

Let's see—twelve-thirty—the eaglet should be nearly dried off by now, I thought.

Looking out over the valley north of the woodland, I daydreamed about how the Apaches and the Cheyennes must have used my lunch spot to hunt deer, antelope, elk, and bison. To the west, north, and east there were no roads, no reservoirs, no cattle—no signs of other men. Even fences were absent in that large tract of open range. It was a panorama in which the junipers and pines stood only on the periphery of the valley.

Back at the rendezvous spot near the Foundation Eyrie, where I was to meet Jack, two o'clock—the specified time—and then three o'clock passed. I was always riding Jack for being a few minutes late in the mornings. Sometimes he would drive home in the evening, spend a few hours with his family, and then drive back to my house to sleep in the driveway—just so he would be there no matter what time I got up.

"Where the hell've you been?" I asked him as he arrived at nearly four o'clock. "The tapes had better be good! Did that egg hatch?"

He looked at me rather scornfully and reminded me that he had no control over when the birds chose to do interesting things. Then, as we headed for town, making several stops to check other nests as we went, he answered all my questions in detail.

"The egg you saw pipping yesterday hatched right on schedule, sometime between seven-thirteen and ten-twenty-seven," he said. "The female stood up at seven-twelve long enough for me to see the two eggs.

The bird was halfway around the shell then and was out the next time the female stood up."

Jack's recollection of the precise times impressed me. He had heard the chick clearly at about nine-twenty—his guess of the time of hatching. Having hatched many raptor eggs in captivity, I knew how boisterous the final release of hatching can be. Each push of a chick's muscles extends it more and more from the fetal position. The crack lengthens as the imprisoned bird turns, pushes with its legs, and tries to raise its head with the aid of a special hatching muscle contracting thick and strong at the back of the neck. Almost free, the chick peeps often and squirms with smallish might to force the broken shell from its back, like a rodeo horse high off the ground struggling to throw its rider.

"The tiercel brought a stick to the nest at ten-twenty-seven," Jack continued, "but he dropped it as soon as the female got up. Then they just stood there for a couple of minutes and stared at the eaglet and the other egg, which had a small hole in it. It'll probably hatch tomorrow."

At hatching, a raptor is a poor gangling excuse for a bird. An eaglet, weighing between three and four ounces, is big-headed and otherwise out of proportion with the dimensions of an adult eagle. When the sparse coat of down feathers is still wet and glued to the bird's pink skin, it is a sight endearing only to another bird, possibly only to another golden eagle.

"When I first saw the eaglet, its eyes were half closed," Jack went on. "It looked like it had a bad case of the blahs. Then it suddenly began squirming and cheeping like crazy, as if it was still trying to get rid of the shell. Finally it stopped, curled up into the fetal position, and fell asleep."

Eyas—nestling—golden eagles, like all eyas raptors, hatch nearly helpless and almost totally dependent upon their parents for food and warmth. They are not completely naked like robins and other perching birds familiar to most people. Nevertheless, the down covering of newly hatched raptors does not effectively insulate them against the cold. Their body temperatures fluctuate with surrounding air temperatures for the first two or three weeks if they are left unbrooded; at first they are partially cold-blooded, like reptiles.

Because of their uncoordinated movements, hatchling raptors have no effective locomotion. On the other hand, precocial birds, such as ducks, geese, and shorebirds, are well coordinated within hours of hatching; they can walk, swim, and feed much like their parents. The activity of a duckling during its first day out of the shell would thoroughly

MOUNTAIN PLOVER

exhaust any recently hatched raptor. Ducklings also possess a thick downy covering that gives them a greater capacity for temperature regulation than relatively naked eaglets.

I gleaned much more from Jack's excellent taped comments. The female eagle flew to the food cache to eat shortly after the male came. In the meantime, the male fulfilled an uncertain obligation: brooding a newly hatched youngster and a hatching egg. During the nestling period, the tiercel was to be only a rare visitor to the eyrie, but he was compelled to make several final attempts at incubation. He addressed his offspring soon after the female departed by walking on limply folded toes to a position directly over them. He stood momentarily, eyes downcast, and then settled onto his charges with the usual teetering motions. Uncertainty, however, was evidenced in his final posture: his tail was depressed lower and his legs were slightly straighter than usual so as not to exert his full weight.

Fortunately, the female soon returned to relieve his quandary, and he hastily relinquished his position. She brought a plucked pheasant, and after placing it on the nest rim she immediately assumed the proper brooding posture. She stood closely over the young bird but did not lie on it as she had the eggs. She stayed there, over her offspring, until about two o'clock. Her mate flew by twice more before then, but kept his distance; his role had changed—to a stepped-up pace of food gathering.

The new eaglet was fed for the first time shortly after two. That was Jack's reason for being late, and the tapes substantiated his story. The eaglet had acquired a more respectable raptorial appearance during its few hours out of the shell. The down feathers had dried and fluffed; they stood straight up on the upper back and head. The mother eagle rose, shuffled to the pheasant, tore it open, and ate at least twenty bites herself before selecting small tender pieces of liver for her hours-old eaglet. The youngster's eyes were open, and it leaned back with its head held shakily high and its beak open—the signs of a healthy chick. Nevertheless, it swallowed only two bites before fatigue precluded further efforts. At that point, the parent eagle resumed brooding and Jack readied for his departure.

Another stage of the eagle life history had passed.

IO

IN SEARCH
OF NEW
ARRIVALS

The only living evidence of a forgotten home, the honey locust tree, grew alongside a collapsed cistern. A small wood-frame shack with a stone foundation lay in ruins fifty feet from the tree. Only a stone henhouse had withstood the punishment of time at Honey Locust Shack. Stones washed down from the Rocky Mountains, although excellent building materials, had made tilling toilsome and slow. Cobbles uncovered during plowing had been carried or carted to piles at the edges of fields. One heap lay about thirty yards north of the tree; another was farther away. Other stones extended in two broken lines to the cement steps that, several decades before, had led to a heavy screen door. Imagining a sun-darkened farm boy rushing out after breakfast into a dusty yard, I could almost hear the hinges creak. The yard would have been full of chickens, one or more dogs, a couple of milk cows, and a sow with a large litter of suckling piglets; the boy might have been just in time to ride with his father on a horse-drawn plow or a steam-driven tractor, out to a twenty-acre plot being conditioned for planting the next spring.

In 1972, though, a rusty wellhead stuck eight inches above the ground, not far from the withering honey locust tree. A windmill had once drawn water from that pipe and then had fed it to the cistern, to a two-acre garden, and to the tree. Litter was everywhere. Pieces of a potbellied stove—which had surely devoured its share of corncobs and dried cow chips—were scattered about. Not a board of the windmill tower remained. Had it been burned by the hapless settlers in a final hopeless attempt to endure a long winter snowstorm isolated by miles of drifted-over prairie?

Often I wished for more time to dig for old bottles or to fit pieces of the ruin together. The steel rim and a few wooden spokes of a wagon wheel were nearly sodded under; yet I could find no other parts of the old prairie schooner or oxcart or hay wagon. Half the hood of an old Ford placed people there during the late twenties, making them certain victims of the next decade's great drought and national depression. Where is the rest of that horseless carriage now? I thought.

Since we were busy with the other species, Jack and I did not look for Swainson's hawks intently until early May, when they were courting and thus more conspicuous than they would be during incubation. Every tree on the study area had to be checked before the cottonwoods leafed out, because scanning leafless trees for nests from a distance with a spotting scope was more expedient than walking to each tree and straining to find nests in thick summer foliage.

Honey Locust Shack was one of the first places I visited on May 2nd in search of Swainson's hawks. I had dropped Jack off several miles south of the Breaks to walk a stretch of sparsely wooded creek bottom, while I trucked from abandoned farmstead to abandoned farmstead to check isolated trees.

I had seen no hawks in passing Honey Locust Shack two days before, on my way to the scarp woodland; neither did I see any at first glance on May 2nd, so I looked more closely for signs of them. No new building materials lay in the nest; no droppings were below the tree or under nearby posts. Perhaps the pair that nested there in 1971 had moved to Antelope Reservoir, where nest building had already begun.

As I walked among the broken relics, a shrill mournful cry sounded an objection to my presence. Soaring almost directly overhead, about three hundred feet high, were the hawks; they had returned after all.

I left quickly, but not before noting their strikingly different plumages. The coloring of Swainson's hawks includes numerous combinations of blacks, grays, whites, and browns. Dark trailing edges of the wings and a bib of dark feathers high on the breast are the most conspicuous field marks of light-colored birds—like the tiercel at Honey

Locust Shack. His mate was much darker; her basic field marks blended almost imperceptibly with other feathers.

But one characteristic of adult Swainson's hawks always identifies them; a small patch of white feathers extends nearly from eye to eye across the top of the beak, though it fades quickly to dark gray on the forehead. The striking contrast makes the patch shine like a headlight and gives an incubating Swainson's hawk away, even when it is lying low and just peering over the nest rim.

Swainson's hawks are generally regarded as tame and confiding, but not too fleet of wing or aggressive in the chase. Their reputation for being slack-mettled—though they are not always so—doubtless comes from their mastery of the art of opportunism and the ease with which they adapt to man. A tree at an abandoned farmstead—or a reservoir—is as good a nesting place as a sparse forest along a dry creek. Telephone poles near busy highways serve well as hunting perches unless there is something better; for example, if a farmer is plowing a nearby field, Swainson's hawks often search the clearing dust behind the tractor until they obtain a cropful of small rodents. Other times, Swainson's hawks walk across a field in search of grasshoppers rather than hunt small mammals from a soar. They are generalized feeders; they kill rabbits, small birds, ground squirrels, many kinds of mice and voles, insects, snakes, and other reptiles, keying on what is easiest to catch.

Thus Swainson's hawks exploit a mix of nature's and man's ways with great success. I recognize this quality just as I do the charisma of an eagle, the beauty of a male kestrel, or the adeptness of a prairie falcon. In being adaptable, opportunistic, and generalized feeders, Swainson's hawks have become the most numerous raptor of the shortgrass prairie.

In the jargon of the locals, the six-mile journey to the next prospective Swainson's hawk nest—near Cattle Pond—was one east, four south, and one east. I crossed two dry creeks and skirted the western edge of five square miles of winter wheat to get there. The crop was well up, but growth was beginning to slow down because rainfall had been far below average during March and April. Similarly, temperatures had averaged several degrees higher each month since the first of the year. The warmer weather accelerated plant development, but the time was rapidly approaching when moisture stored in the ground would be so depleted as to limit growth, particularly that of the late-season grasses and forbs.

Standing at the crossroads near Cattle Pond and looking up a gentle three-and-a-half-mile slope toward the Eagle Breaks, I could see many different plant communities with borders as straight as surveyor's lines. The difference was often striking from one side of a trail or a fence to the other, the result of staggered abandonment of cultivated fields through the years.

Past land use dictates where specific plant associations occur; the plants then determine which animals live on a particular acre; and, finally, the presence of suitable prey animals attracts raptors of one or more species. If vegetation is stripped away by fire, flood, or the plow, and the violated land is allowed to go back, a long series of ecological steps are required before the best-suited plants (and the animals that go with them) are restored. Secondary ecological succession, the natural rehabilitation of disturbed land, is an important part of the ecology of most shortgrass prairie; it explains the patchwork of plant communities near the Eagle Breaks.

Attesting to this, there were the rich green wheat fields I had just passed. As long as cultivation continues there, native plants will be crowded out and rehabilitation will not begin. Every attempt to do so will be aborted by the next plowing and planting.

Adjacent to the cultivated land was a half square mile left fallow for three years. Kangaroo rats, pocket gophers, and other burrowing rodents abounded in loose soil near the edges of that field. Away from the edges, the ground was dotted only with annual plants—mostly Russian thistle and common sunflowers—that grew from new seeds each year like most farm crops. But in their cultivated fields farmers stack the soil in favor of their own plantings; they consider wild annuals noxious weeds because they spread rapidly into abandoned or improperly farmed land. Russian thistle, a "tumbler," drops seeds everywhere on its fence-to-fence, wind-driven journeys to disseminate its kind. In the restoration of abandoned fields, thistles, sunflowers, and other annuals play an important role: they begin to stabilize the soil for the next stage of succession. Besides, sunflower seeds are an important food of mourning doves and many smaller birds.

According to the local rancher, the land east of the wheat fields had been abandoned for at least eight years. The same annuals were there, along with lamb's-quarter and a few other new ones. Most important, perennial forbs had become established. Perennial plants develop each summer from parts—usually roots—that persist through the winter. Thus slimflower scurf pea and scarlet globe mallow were the first indications of year-to-year stabilization of the soil. Several species of grasses

also moved in, but they were not dominant eight years after the last plowing; neither were the shrubs, such as fourwing saltbush and broom snakeweed, that appeared for the first time. Among the dominant birds and mammals were meadowlarks, horned larks, cottontails, black-tailed jackrabbits, pocket gophers, and many smaller rodents.

Land higher on the slope, close to the Breaks and near Honey Locust Shack, had been idle for more than a decade. A change was evident from perennial forbs to perennial midgrasses—foxtail barley, Indian ricegrass, and western wheatgrass. Grazing became profitable. The number of Russian thistle plants decreased, while globe mallow and scurf pea increased. Plains prickly pear was present, as were the shrubs that appeared during the preceding stage of succession. Lark buntings and chestnut-collared longspurs nested in the best stands of midgrasses, and thirteen-lined ground squirrels were there in small numbers.

Most land south of the Breaks was dominated by more permanent grasses, particularly red three-awn, blue grama, and buffalo grass. Red three-awn is the most important grass during the second and third decades after abandonment. A gradual infiltration of sod grasses finally occurs, and other species of forbs—aster, crypthantha, and pale evening primrose—move in. Common winter fat joins the shrub flora, and yucca becomes well established.

During the third to fifth decades after a field is abandoned, it is recognizable as shortgrass prairie. The land within a few hundred yards of the Breaks—where cultivation was never profitable—was exemplary; there were also a few large tracts that had always been used for grazing. Such a pasture extended from Cattle Pond south and east downstream to the Cottonwood Eyrie and beyond. This stage of succession is reached when the spreading shortgrass sod dominates other grasses. Many midgrasses persist, but most are less abundant than during the lengthy three-awn stage. The forb populations, which include a few plants each of many types, fluctuate in numbers—sometimes in response to the amount of rainfall in the preceding autumn, other times to the conditions of spring. With the continuous shortgrass sod come mountain plovers, McCown's longspurs, grasshopper mice, white-tailed jackrabbits, and more thirteen-lined ground squirrels, although lark buntings, horned larks, and meadowlarks remain the dominant birds.

There is much more I need to learn about the plant associations of the shortgrass prairie, primarily because I was very slow to develop a consuming interest in them. I had known only the forests and mountains of Alaska and Washington during my recallable past. My cottonwoods were spruces, birches, and Douglas firs; my saltbushes were Scotch broom and huckleberries; and grasses were just something that cattle ate.

Today I am quite fond of buffalo grass and slimflower scurf pea—or, at least, I appreciate more that hawks eat the animals that eat such plants.

The wide-open spaces appeal to me now; to my delight, the camp-grounds near the Eagle Breaks are left empty while thousands of people drive across the prairie to the crowded forests of the Rockies. They can have the woodlands, jammed highways, and commercial resorts of the mountains; forests constrain me now, although I would enjoy learning more about the less disturbed ones. The horizon-to-horizon sky on the prairie seems to invite bird study, while a forest canopy is a natural "No Trespassing" sign one always wants to breach. I cannot lie on my back among the trees and watch an eagle courting—at least not for very long. A forest couches its animals in secrecy; the prairie displays them!

The tree containing the hawks' nest at Cattle Pond did not actually fit the scheme of ecological succession on the shortgrass prairie. As a seed-ling, its chance of survival would have been very small if it had not been nurtured by some homesteader. Sadly, the tree, a fifty-foot cottonwood, stands alone today because it cannot reproduce: seedlings are always eaten or trampled by cattle, antelope, rabbits, or other plant-eating animals. The rogue survives only by gathering water from the pond through long deep roots. As the pond shrinks toward a small earthen dam every August and September, the entire prairie becomes a brown tinderbox. Exposed mud dries, cracks, and crumbles to dust after being seared by the sun and trodden by cattle. Eventually, the cottonwood tree will be unable to withstand the seasonal dehydration and will die. Raptors will be forced to nest elsewhere or they may just stop breeding, unable to find another nest site in the treeless expanse of their chosen territory.

All this did not apply to the pair of hawks I saw soaring silently above the old tree; they probably would not witness its demise in their lifetime. Both wheeled in progressively higher quarter-mile circles borne by unflexed wings for minutes at a time.

One bird—I assume the male—soared to a position directly over the nest, set his wings in a slightly bent attitude, and glided off toward the Breaks. He lost most of his altitude in the first mile and again began a leisurely ringing soar back toward the nest, crisscrossing below the flight path of his mate many times. After several minutes, he finally reached her altitude and began flapping vigorously and flying in tight circles, a marked contrast to the idle soaring of the preceding fifteen minutes.

Repeatedly he climbed ten feet, stalled out, dived thirty feet or so, and then immediately climbed back skyward to his original altitude, as if flying up a circular staircase; his wing linings flashed like white flags in the sun. Again at his mate's altitude, he resumed circling like a tetherball at the end of a fifteen-foot string. It seemed as though his centrifugal force would push him into larger circles; finally, it did, but he quickly maneuvered himself into a vertical climb—his body axis straight up and down—and stalled out again, following with a long delicate swoop to the previous year's nest, which still hung in shambles near the top center of the old cottonwood, not in the most weather-wise position.

The final, rocketing climb was launched from horizontal flight in a tight circle, rather than as a follow-through of a dive—behavior I had never seen or read about before. He seemed to defy gravity like no other hawk I have ever seen! From then on, I had more respect for the aerial abilities of Swainson's hawks; they are not as slack-mettled as some believe.

Previously, discussions of Swainson's hawks had often led to humorous stories: they are the clowns of misfortune among raptors. I have seen young ones fly to trees and end up perched like fruit bats—hanging underneath a limb. Unable to right themselves, they finally drop unceremoniously to the ground. Both young and adults commonly perch on telephone wires, their toes wrapped tightly around the wire more than once, trying to stop the precarious wobble that usually overtakes them, much the same as rough-legged hawks do in winter. I fully expect someday to see a Swainson's hawk hanging underneath a wire by clenched feet seemingly out of communication with the brain of the hapless creature.

The Swainson's hawk's method of grasshopper slaughter is also laughable. They often kill hoppers by running after them—not by flying—and then squashing the bite-sized prey by spasmodically clenching their feet. Are there other animals that chew with their feet?

The courtship flight was sufficient evidence of nesting activity, so I marked another nest site on the field map and proceeded south and west several miles to pick up Jack and to search for more trees and other pairs of hawks. In passing, I glassed Raven Tree. A ferruginous hawk,

peering from just above the nest rim, was visible only under thirty-power magnification. There were no fresh tire tracks on the short trail to the nest; unlike the happenings at Cattle Pond, everything was quiet.

Later, driving along and eating lunch, I told Jack about the Swainson's hawk courtship flight. He had found another owl nest and three more pairs of Swainson's hawks himself, but our conversation was dominated by a discussion of reproductive strategies of the two prairie buteos.

"Why would Swainson's hawks have such spectacular courtship behavior when we've never seen anything like that in ferrugs except attacks on other raptors?" I asked Jack, baiting him to see if he would swallow a new thought of mine.

"I don't know," he said. "I haven't given it much thought."

"Why do ferrugs build such large nests?" I continued.

"They're large birds," he answered.

"Yeah, but if you compare Swainson's and ferruginous nests, the size difference is out of proportion to the difference in the size of the birds," I said, convinced that he had not beaten me to my thoughts.

Then I went on to answer my own questions, not in the detail that has developed since that May day, but with the same logic. The facts were not new; it was just the way in which they were put together to draw some inferences.

First of all, one basic difference in the breeding cycles of ferruginous and Swainson's hawks is the length of time each spends on its breeding grounds. Ferruginous hawks are relatively sedentary in the midwestern Great Plains; Swainson's hawks are highly migratory. As a rule, resident birds have more time available for breeding than migrants. In one hundred and seventy-five days, Swainson's hawks must go through courtship, build nests, lay two to four eggs, incubate for about thirty-five days, rear young in the nest for at least thirty-eight days, attend to young for several weeks after fledging, and prepare themselves for the long time-consuming fall migration back to the pampas of South America.

According to one theory, in prehistoric times Swainson's hawks or their ancestors (which probably came from South America in the first place) were naturally forced out of their northern breeding range each fall by a dearth of prey. When grasshoppers die in the fall and other food sources are relatively unavailable, Swainson's hawks must leave North America. Those that tended to move back south were selected for over thousands of years. They found another source of insects, young rodents, and fledgling birds during summer in the Southern Hemi-

sphere. Today the migratory behavior of Swainson's hawks is so highly evolved that they actually prepare for the journey. Each one eats thousands of grasshoppers during late August and September—a helping hand that most farmers fail to recognize. Small fat deposits throughout their bodies are glutted for later use as energy sources during the long southward flight.

The same evolutionary time was apparently used by ferruginous hawks to adapt to the rigors of winter in the Northern Hemisphere. Having probably immigrated from Asia, rather than from South America, they or their ancestors may have already been adapted to cold. In any event, only short seasonal movements are now necessary—hundreds rather than thousands of miles. We do not know how far south the adult ferruginous hawks that nest near the Eagle Breaks travel, but their young move as far as central Mexico; young birds generally disperse farther than adults. We do know that ferruginous hawks live near the Breaks all winter, are on breeding territories by late February or early March, and begin laying eggs five to six weeks later. By comparison, Swainson's hawks migrate south, return directly to their traditional nest sites, and begin laying within just two or three weeks.

I knew that all this made sense to Jack, because he was fairly quiet when I presented it the first time. We must have tried a thousand new thoughts on each other that summer; silence was as good as an approving nod, while poor ideas were always attacked immediately. But the atmosphere for learning was casual, something I rarely felt in school.

Before I had finished my discourse, we came across another pair of Swainson's hawks setting up housekeeping in a box elder tree not ten feet from an improved dirt road. The male hawk was on the ground, but soon the female flew over him, perched on a nearby fence post, and began preening.

"Looks like a come-on to me," I said.

"Yeah, but which one is which?" Jack asked. "The bird on the ground must be the male."

"Can't be sure, I guess, but it seems to be looking for something."

"How about nest material?" Jack said sarcastically.

"How about a grasshopper lunch?" I countered.

Often a bird's motive is unclear until one sees the end result. Patient observation is often rewarded with understanding if one follows an animal to the end of a behavioral sequence. These comments, tape-recorded at the time, answered many of our questions:

> "The bird (male) runs in quick little strides, stops, and then looks back at the other bird (female). It reaches down often, but does not get a stick each time. The action appears like a bluffing activity. It picked up one stick in its mouth, dropped it, ran a few more steps, and again looked back at the other bird."

"There it goes," Jack said in the background as I shut off the microphone.

I continued taping when the sequence had ended, knowing for certain then which Swainson's hawk was the male:

> "The male flew from the ground to the back of the female, and they copulated. He appeared to be carrying something as he approached her. Instead, it was just his feet; two or three yards before he got to her, he already had them clenched and out in front in order to land without clawing her. The balling of the feet was like I have seen incubating birds do, trying not to crush their eggs with widespread toes.
>
> "The male stayed on for six to eight seconds; there wasn't

too much passing of the tail underneath. It was a rather abortive attempt; but then, one wouldn't expect Swainson's hawks to do anything very well! The male then flew five or six fence posts away, and the female jumped down to the ground directly below the fence post she was on. She then picked up a small stick and climbed at a thirty-degree angle up to the nest."

Our patience had been duly rewarded. When we drove off, we knew the sex of the birds, that the male was not looking for a grasshopper lunch, and that the female's sashaying and preening were parts of her courtship behavior. In fact, the male was not even looking for nest material. His puttering with sticks was equivalent to her preening; both were displacement activities, behaviors out of context with what was about to happen.

Driving idly toward another grove of trees, I continued my discourse on the reproductive strategies of Swainson's and ferruginous hawks. My next point—again nothing original or that Jack did not already know—was that although photoperiod or day length has been shown to be an extremely important stimulant for breeding in many birds, courtship flights, nest building, territorial conflict, and other pre-incubation behaviors also help effect the internal changes in hormonal levels necessary for breeding. But each type of nesting activity, depending on the species, plays a greater or lesser role as a stimulant for breeding.

Take courtship displays and nest-building behavior as examples. Swainson's hawks perform spectacular aerial gymnastics, as at Cattle Pond and several other places where Jack and I have since seen the behavior. Swainson's hawks also make pugnacious defenses of their territories, particularly against owls, as at Antelope Reservoir. Nest building by Swainson's hawks is also intense and relatively short-lived. Such vigorous activity may be the quickest way to add the necessary stimulation (above the effects of day length) for mating and egg-laying.

Thus in highly migratory species there may be a sharp rise in certain hormonal levels that peaks out and then drops slowly. This possibility is supported by the fact that the highly migratory buteos—Swainson's hawks and, in eastern North America, broad-winged hawks—are the most diligent carriers of green material to their nests during incubation and nestling growth. I assume that green material is brought after egg-laying as a carry-over of hormonally controlled nest building. Migratory birds apparently are slaves to a spike in their hormonal levels at mating time.

Ferruginous hawks, on the other hand, seem to receive more of the necessary stimulation for breeding from nest building, and their nests are large as a result. I have never seen, heard of, or read about a courtship performance of ferruginous hawks that I would call extraordinary or acrobatic. Nests are such a fetish to them, however, that two or more are visited and repaired each year, as with the pair at Raven Tree. This is common among resident diurnal raptors, including golden eagles. Migrants do not have the time required to spend working on two nests every year.

In building larger, sturdier nests over a longer period of time than Swainson's hawks, ferruginous hawks seem to be readied for mating steadily but more slowly. As a result, the spike in their hormonal levels may be lower (and the residual effect slight after egg-laying). Ferruginous hawks do not bring as much fresh nest material after eggs are laid as Swainson's hawks do.

One would be hard pressed in a lifetime to amass all the facts necessary to prove or refute these ideas conclusively. Such is another dilemma brought by years of education. Learning, like life, is time-limited; the desire to learn too soon exceeds the potential of one's years. Although increased awareness gained through education offsets many of the constraints of looking at life with a scientific eye, the choice of which curiosities to pursue can be perplexing—indeed, disappointing.

Why *do* Swainson's hawks have such spectacular courtship behavior?

11

NAÏVE HOPES

Unlike the sandstone-and-conglomerate cliff at the Foundation Eyrie, erosion near the Oil Well Eyrie had long ago destroyed the cap rock above light-colored silts and clays laid down up to six hundred feet thick in places. During the Oligocene Epoch, between forty million and twenty-five million years ago, uncountable numbers of prehistoric animals—of hundreds of species—died and fell to the muddy bottoms of ancient lakes and temporary ponds. Through geologic time, their bones were preserved under more layers of silt. During recent times, fossil turtles, iguanas, vultures, hawks, cormorants, plovers, rabbits, rodents, carnivorous mammals, and superb remains of hoofed mammals, such as swine, rhinoceroses, camels, and horses, have been unearthed by stream flow within a few miles of the Eagle Breaks. In the course of our studies in the area, we learned just where to find fossils: an old railroad trestle for snails; one creek bed for oysters, another for clams, still another for leaf imprints; and the cliffs for vertebrate animals.

We arrived at the Oil Well Eyrie about eight-twenty in brilliant morning sunshine. By then—May 14th—Jack and I had found nearly fifty pairs of Swainson's hawks and about a hundred pairs of other raptors near potential nest sites—more than half of the two hundred and fifty nests we studied that summer. Except for great horned owls and the Foundation Eyrie eagles, though, we knew little about nest success or failure. We had disturbed only a few easily observed pairs of each species to allow proper timing of our later visits to the majority of nests. Dates of important events at the undisturbed sites were determined by recording the ages of all nestlings on the first nest visit after hatching, and later calculating backward to egg-laying dates, using average incubation times.

Although it was sunny that morning, the four previous days had been cloudy, foggy, and plagued by thunderstorms. Yet only two-thirds of an inch of rain had fallen in most places—not much for a thirsty prairie. The back trails remained traversable except for a few short detours around water-filled ruts. We also had to detour slightly to cross the creek downstream from the eyrie because of a trickle of water, the first I had ever seen flowing there. As Jack drove wide open across the soft creek bed, I noticed the grass lying bent downstream and covered with silt where water had coursed as much as ten feet wide in places. More than two-thirds of an inch of rain had fallen there or somewhere upstream during the recent storms.

We parked near the wellhead where the pops and sputters of an unsteady pump motor echoing against thirty vertical feet of bluff drowned out all other sounds. An ugly sludge pit and greasy odors detracted from the delight of being near an eagle eyrie. In the sludge, a duck lay oil-soaked and half submerged, put to a sticky death by an abuse of its habitat—a common occurrence wherever the oil industry blights the prairie.

And no eagles plied their usual domain! I felt the chill of emptiness in my back. Had the presence of the well—the coming and going of its attendants—caused a greater tragedy by forcing the eagles to desert? At least, the eagles had made an effort to coexist with the noisy steel monstrosity in continuous motion below their nest.

We climbed above the creek bed, our footing uncertain in loose sand and silt, and found most of the nest lying below the small bluff, not in the lofty position overlooking the hollow where I had seen it before. I cursed the oilmen, wishing no less than the sludge pit for them. Why doesn't man try to coexist with wildlife by developing natural resources in ways that are more in concert with nature? I thought. The incessant dirge of the pump bespoke decades of haste to do just the opposite.

Jack searched the nest ruins, which trailed at least fifteen feet down the sloping lower portion of the bank, while I climbed up a gentler part of the bluff to reach the actual nest site. Deep in the fallen sticks Jack found shattered eggshells and, finally, two almost fully developed embryos. What a waste!

But evidence atop the bluff—to my surprise—vindicated the oil-men, at least for the destruction of the eagle eggs. The fossil-bearing loose clay-and-silt banks of the western Great Plains are only marginal nest sites for golden eagles. With sites at a premium, however, some eagles are forced to use them. All I could do was reconstruct the *natural* demise of the nest.

Sometime before that breeding season, perhaps many years before, runoff from heavy rains had been channeled and had begun cascading over the bank, much as the creek below had done after a deluge, thousands of years before, near Battle Gap six miles southeast. The water fell about five feet at the Oil Well Eyrie onto a hard-packed layer of clay before cascading again. That washed out a footing where a nest could be placed during drier times.

But water flows in the same channels once they are established. Because of the fitfulness of prairie weather, several breeding seasons passed between the construction of the nest and its flooding; the mass of sticks attested to the nest's age. But the female had no way of knowing that a drenching rain would come at the wrong time in 1972 or that the runoff would be funneled onto her back. The case was closed except for the despair of trying, in the mind's eye, to develop methods of preventing such nest failures in the future.

It is not that saving every eaglet would be important to golden eagle population dynamics; they have lived with such disasters for millennia. About one out of every four eagle eggs never hatches, as a rule; more die as nestlings. But, being a naturalist, just as I strive for good field technique, I hope for near perfection from nature. This is a naïve hope, though, which, if I had the wisdom of Thoreau or Burroughs, or the experience of Errington, I would surely abandon. There is no guarantee of annual success; failure is part of life's scheme; a predator's misfortune is the prey's advantage; and that advantage is soon shifted to the predators. The pendulum of nature swings. Yet I still contemplate improving the raptor's lot. A wasted eaglet is more than I care to concede.

The next stop on our itinerary was the Foundation Eyrie. There was very little conversation en route until, almost simultaneously, we broke the silence.

"Why not put an artificial nest structure on top of that bluff?" I said.

"I was thinking of an old wooden windmill tower," Jack said. "They'd take it in a minute."

For some time, Jack and I had been optimistic about population management of birds of prey. The more we thought about it, the more the potential loomed. When we later looked at our data on nearly fifty eagle nests, we found about a third of them inadequate or vulnerable to failure. Some pairs of eagles built nests every year, but for unknown reasons the nests always fell. Why not put sturdy wooden platforms in their favored trees for them to nest on? Other pairs were continually harassed by passers-by. Why not post the land and keep people away? And we never did find a successful eagle nest on a creek bank like the Oil Well Eyrie. I know of half a dozen other spots for old wooden windmill towers that would suit the purpose.

There are also many miles of prairie where *no* nest sites are available for eagles—or any other raptor, for that matter. Why must birds of prey, or any wildlife, depend so heavily on the fortuitous lay of the land for breeding habitat? Nest sites for raptors are clumped along cliff lines and creeks; they must be spread out for birds of prey to make the fullest use of wild lands. Why not create new (or rehabilitate old) breeding habitat in barren prairies? It made sense for game species, such as pronghorn antelope and game birds. Why not do the same for nongame species?

We drove the four miles to the Foundation Eyrie in less than ten minutes despite the poor roads. Walking from the truck to the eyrie was easier in daylight and unimpeded by the tools, comforts, and food required for a whole day of observation from the blind. One of the parent eagles was soaring high above us from the moment we stepped out of the truck. It watched our approach with concern—welcome concern after the Oil Well Eyrie episode. By the time we arrived atop the nest cliff, two eagles wheeled overhead.

I crawled the last eighty feet to the blind to observe the young birds for a few moments before disturbing them. Jack lay down on his back some distance away and watched the adults. My secretiveness was unnecessary; both eyases were asleep, with legs tucked underneath them, wings drooped, and heads rested on the side of the nest cup. They were unaware of the danger evidenced by their parents' behavior. Nearly full crops and the warmth of an early-May midmorning sun tranquilized them; sleep comes rapidly to sated eyases.

Each weighed about two pounds—eight to ten times their hatching weights—at two weeks of age. Doubtless they were still brooded. In cold, a female eagle will nudge her eaglets back under her; but she will allow them to struggle free and crawl out if the temperature is moderate. And she will even leave them unattended for short periods. If her charges cannot reach shade, however, or if a storm comes, she returns quickly to tent them. Twenty or twenty-five days after hatching, it is physically impossible for young golden eagles to be brooded; they are too large. Then the female, when not actually feeding her offspring, spends much of her time perched on the nest rim.

Not only did the sleepy eaglets have full crops that day; they also had a full larder. Flies buzzed around a small pile of prey, mostly rabbits, on the far edge of the nest. Farther away, the cliff swallows busied themselves building nests out of mud left after the recent rainstorms. Some ambitious ones had completed their adobe huts, while others stood in partially roofed openings that gaped widely at the outdoors. Still others were perched on just the floors of their recently started nests. All the

CLIFF SWALLOWS

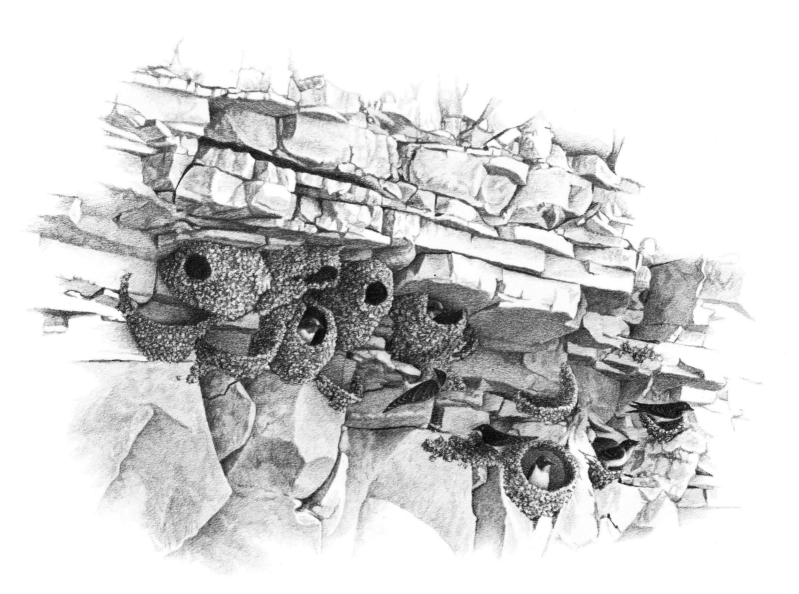

local residents—eagles, swallows, and house sparrows—were doing satisfactorily.

After a few minutes in the blind, I came out, and Jack joined me in walking to the edge of the cliff.

"The adults are still hanging up there," Jack said, pointing them out again. "They were a little farther north for a while, but they've never gone out of sight."

Timidness, not aggressiveness, is the normal reaction of golden eagles to direct human intrusion into the vicinity of their eyries. Some say that their reaction represents aloofness, but those who do must never have looked up to see the concerned parents wheeling overhead. The adults over the Foundation Eyrie were so high that I could see them only when they banked and presented a broad silhouette.

Several feet to one side of the eyrie, I peered over the cliff expecting to see both eaglets rear back on their tarsi and open their beaks in fear. Instead, they just lay there; they could see me, but neither fear nor threat reactions had developed.

The eyrie was high on the cliff; the nest rim could almost be reached with the fingertips if one assumed a prone position and leaned over the precipice. In that way, I finally got one of the eaglets to rear back in response to my hand dangling just above its head. Apparently, the vision of young raptors is confined to the nest area for a few days after hatching. One researcher even tested the pupillary reflex of golden eagles, much the same as an eye doctor would test a man's. At ten days of age, the eaglet's reaction was inferior to that of an adult eagle, but the discrepancy disappeared by the time the eaglet was twenty-four days old. Evidently, the visual ability of young birds of prey develops gradually.

We had not brought ropes to the Foundation Eyrie, because our only goals were to confirm the eaglets' good health and to record prey items. No fewer than twelve hind feet of rabbits lay in the nest, from one adult and two young cottontails, two large black-tailed jackrabbits, and one unidentifiable young jackrabbit. In addition, feathers of a hen pheasant and two tails of thirteen-lined ground squirrels were on the nest rim. Three of the rabbit carcasses were fresh; two were partially eaten but beginning to rot; the other was picked clean.

Through the centuries, in addition to myths about eagles attacking people, another falsehood has been passed from generation to generation: the eagles' urge to kill. While Jack and I pondered ways to conserve golden eagles, a respected journalist—with his mass-media outlets—wrote an editorial that justified shooting and poisoning of eagles because of their insatiable blood lust that drives them to kill one lamb or rabbit after another and leave them to rot.

When that misinformation reached the newsstands, it was not difficult to see where our hope to put a nest structure above the Oil Well Eyrie stood: too many people would believe the man with the pen, who probably had never even seen a golden eagle.

What about the pile of food beginning to rot in the Foundation Eyrie? Such was a common occurrence. Do birds of prey waste food—even if they are not possessed by an uncontrollable penchant for blood-letting, as some would have you believe?

Raptors often kill larger prey than they can consume in one meal. During the summer, an adult eagle eats about a half-pound of food each day, depending on its sex, the weather, its level of activity, and many other factors. A full-grown cottontail weighs between two and three pounds, a black-tailed jackrabbit twice that. This normally leads to a certain amount of waste, although birds often return to a kill several times, and both birds of a pair may feed from the same carcass.

The heaviest overkill, and perhaps the only serious excess, occurs during the breeding season just after hatching. As eyases grow, more food is brought but less is wasted. After the young can feed themselves, virtually everything carried to the nest is picked clean. Yet I have seen a brood of newly hatched Swainson's hawks surrounded by seven dead lark buntings, one kangaroo rat, and one young plover, some of which were rotting. And I have found two hatchling red-tailed hawks literally resting on a veritable commissary of twenty ground squirrels, seven small black-tailed jackrabbits, and one fledgling meadowlark—more food than forty small hawks could eat in a day.

Doubtless the red-tails were overindulgent, but a small quantity of extra food in the nest when eyases are very young has advantages. For example, the eaglets at the Foundation Eyrie were just over a week old when the rainstorms destroyed the Oil Well Eyrie. Exposure to the dampness or lack of food for three or four days could have killed them, too. The amount of rain was apparently great near the Breaks, and it undoubtedly kept rabbits and ground squirrels in their burrows and hideouts. It also lessened their vulnerability to predation, thereby severely testing the hunting ability of the tiercel golden eagle at a time when the female was bound to her brooding responsibilities.

Thus I do not begrudge birds of prey an apparent excess of food when their young are small; their overindulgence is temporary and it probably has survival value. Even where the red-tail nest was heaped with ground squirrels, the rodents were overabundant and needed control. In either case, overkill is justified.

The Indian Eyrie was next after our brief inspection of the Foundation Eyrie. Both parent eagles escorted us to the east gate, just as the tiercel had done with the rancher and his son fifteen days before. It was barely an escort, though; they remained three or four thousand feet high.

As we drove on, Jack began talking about the red-letter day we had had on May 11th.

"You know," he said, "the thing about seeing those three peregrine falcons the other day was not so much the observations as it was the circumstances. Before then, it wasn't clear to me what route arctic peregrines took on spring migration."

"I guess the question is whether they follow the flyways and beaches, as they seem to do in the fall," I said, "or whether they move north along a broad front."

"Right—and for us to see three in one day on the shortgrass prairie—in the spring! Hell, that must be like seeing thirty in a day on the Texas beaches in the fall. There's no flyway out here."

"I suppose I wasn't too impressed the other day because I had seen so many spring peregrines at Creamer's Dairy that time," I admitted.

"Yeah, but that's different; in Fairbanks you were damned near their nesting cliffs," Jack said.

Arctic peregrines winter as far south as Argentina and breed in Alaska, Canada, and Greenland. That requires thousands of miles of migration. No peregrines nest in shortgrass prairie, but peregrines of a different subspecies—*anatum* peregrines—nest in the Rocky Mountains. These may also be seen hunting on the grasslands during their nonnesting seasons, but in late spring they are in breeding territories.

Jack had not been pleased that I wanted to stick with finding more Swainson's hawk nests that drizzly May 11th when the peregrines were about. We had left town at about seven. After an hour of heading east trying to get out from under the fog and mist, Jack had suddenly slammed on the brakes and stopped abruptly in the middle of the highway—not a wise thing to do, but a customary practice of ardent bird watchers.

"What are you trying to do, get us killed?" I cried over the clatter of soda cans in the truck bed and the crash of cameras, scopes, maps, notebooks, and other paraphernalia flying through the cab.

I looked up from my unending toil, the field notebook, to see a dark bird flying with winnowing wingbeats just above the ground.

"I saw it in the rear-view mirror!" Jack exclaimed.

The bird floated along like a marsh hawk, although a bit faster.

"Big deal," I said, questioning his sanity at making such a to-do.

When one tries to focus rapidly on something outside a moving car after one has been reading or writing, it takes a few seconds for the eyes to sort out the stomach. Jack was quick to tell me what was happening.

"Over there, Dr. Olendorff, is a peregrine falcon hunting just like they do on the coastal beaches—by imitating marsh hawks."

It was one of his profound revelations, this time given with obvious excitement. Peregrines are Jack's first love as far as wild creatures go. When I had full use of my senses, the aplomb of a peregrine falcon in flight—or just sitting—flashed in my eyes like the dandy plumage of a male kestrel or the immensity and might of a golden eagle.

A few seconds later, the falcon broke into full-speed pursuit of a horned lark that rose sharply about five feet, just enough to draw the falcon up; then the potential prey dropped to the ground. The falcon could not react that rapidly; it skyed up fifteen to twenty feet, and then continued in the same direction, disappearing into a dark northern sky.

Just that quickly, the topic of conversation for the day was selected.

"I've only seen one other peregrine out here," I said. "It was in May, too; two years ago and only about five miles from here."

"On the grasslands I've seen about six in twelve years," Jack said as he drove on east, more slowly than before and doubtless hoping to see another falcon.

Peregrines are different in many ways from prairie falcons; they are larger and darker—particularly on their heads, which are helmeted in black—and have relatively shorter tails and more powerful wingbeats than do prairie falcons. Both are capable of spectacular diving strikes on prey, but peregrines more often kill ducks and other birds on the wing, while prairie falcons prey heavily on ground squirrels and birds they can force to the ground and catch there.

Less than fifteen miles farther east, we ran into a pelting rainstorm and a moderately dense fog.

Understandably, Jack said, "It's about time to see another peregrine, sitting on a fence post. They wouldn't be flying in this mess."

LONG-BILLED CURLEW

He was not about to abandon his apparently naïve hope as we turned onto a well-traveled dirt road. Moreover, he had fully developed one of his better "instant analyses." The extensive weather front had rolled up from the south, pushing many birds ahead of it—lark buntings, upland plovers, long-billed curlews, and many more American avocets. But what if these migrating birds were caught in the storm? That was Jack's train of thought.

Less than thirty seconds after he had said that peregrines would not be flying in the rain, we came upon a beautiful adult female peregrine on a fence post beside the road. Jack had the clarity of mind not to apply the brakes: that would have scared her. We drove by within twenty feet, continued out of sight over a small rise, turned around, and drove back.

But it was not all that businesslike. We looked and acted anything but professional.

"Get the long lens for the camera!" Jack shouted at the top of his lungs, looking desperately for film on a dashboard loaded with bull horns, moss agate, fossils, a large arrowhead, a few soda cans, eagle feathers, birdbands, sunglasses, and other objects.

At some point, we changed seats without getting out of the truck,

so that Jack could snap pictures as we drove by a second time. The bird was quite cooperative. She did not show us anything spectacular, except herself, but she did make Jack's analysis of the time of year, the weather, and peregrine behavior seem quite perceptive.

Before day's end, after the sun broke through and dried the country-side considerably, we saw a third peregrine many miles farther east. It was perched on a small but sheer cliff that we checked for prairie falcons. Seeing the peregrine, we knew that no prairies nested nearby. There would have been a battle royal, as peregrines and prairies rarely mix.

To round out our successful day of watching the migration of un-common raptors, on the way back west we stopped at a small reservoir we called the Duck Ponds to search nearby trees for nests. There we saw an osprey hunt for several minutes and then catch a foot-long carp on its first plunge. It flew to a large dead cottonwood and ate the fish while we looked on.

Those were the highlights of the day. We also found seven new Swainson's hawk nests, two more pairs of great horned owls, and two new ferruginous-hawk nests—all anticlimactic, of course, to seeing three wild peregrines in one day.

A week later, on May 18th, when Jack saw the same type of weather system developing, he tried to get me to stop at the Duck Ponds. I was still preoccupied with the thousand-square-mile intensive study area, so he drove back nearly fifty miles to the ponds after dropping me off at home at the end of a full day on the grasslands. There, in evening twilight, he photographed the peregrine he intuitively felt would be sitting in the old cottonwood. In 1973, he did the same thing with two of our friends along. They had seen several upland plovers and long-billed curlews one mid-May afternoon. At the Duck Ponds, that evening, there were two feeding peregrines, one on the ground and one in the same cottonwood.

YUCCA PLANT

12

NATURAL
PROBLEMS

Late-morning sun filled the Indian Eyrie when we visited it on May 14th. The tiercel eagle was sitting on a room-sized rock that had long ago fallen away from the cliff. Undercut by rapid erosion of a silt layer, that part of the cap rock broke off, tumbled onto its face, and then slid halfway down a gentle slope toward the prairie before coming to rest. The highest point of the rock was completely whitewashed, indicating its frequent use by birds. The eagle added another daub of whitewash and flew secretively off to the east along the cliff. He saw the potential danger first: our truck.

Jack and I pulled into view of the eyrie and stopped three hundred yards out on the prairie. The female eagle was sitting on the nest rim with one wing extended and drooped; the eaglets were probably in the shade of her wing, their crops bulging with rabbit flesh from the last meal. Countless acres of grassland lay below the eagle family. The countryside was green with accelerated springtime growth and was quiet except for the songs of birds. A meadowlark, dwarfed in size but not in voice by the vast surroundings, had already commandeered the tiercel eagle's sentinel rock as a yodeling perch. Horned larks were courting; a few already had eggs, but their peak egg-laying period was a week or two away. All small birds seemed busy making up for the days when sunshine was rare and the temperature stayed below sixty degrees.

"The lark buntings sure have moved in during the last few days," Jack said as we got out of the truck and began walking toward the eyrie.

"Yeah, most of them must have come ahead of the same storm that brought the peregrines," I said.

Lark buntings are the most numerous of feathered creatures that nest near the Eagle Breaks. They are also among the best songsters. As is done with Swainson's hawks, there is always an exchange of field notes between local bird watchers to determine who spots the first one each year. The earliest flocks of buntings are dominated by males, which are black with striking white wing patches—epaulettes. As May passes, the sex ratio evens out and the males begin courting. Black-and-white wings carry them skyward thirty feet or so whence they half sail, half flutter diagonally to the ground, singing melodiously all the while. Such flights attract mates and announce territorial ownership to other males.

Female lark buntings are easily distinguished from their mates—as well as from females of other species—by their basically brown coloration, spotted breasts, and cream-colored epaulettes. They usually build nests flush with the sod, mostly in patches of midgrasses or near shrubs. Tall plants conceal them from predators and give protection from windstorms and direct sunlight.

As we walked toward the cliff, Jack and I shouted a few times, whistled, clapped, and talked loudly. It was no great ruckus, just assurance that the element of surprise was absent from our approach. It is far better for parent birds to see and hear a threatening advance. This is particularly true of the more timid nest defenders like golden eagles. One can startle a prairie falcon or a great horned owl—even on eggs—and they will turn to fight. Swainson's hawks also defend their eggs vigorously. But golden eagles just hang overhead; ferruginous hawks show the same tendency, although they will actively defend older young on occasion. These shyer birds, which also abandon their nests more readily than the others, seem less able to cope with sudden fright. The naturalist must act accordingly, so that he can always leave a nest with a clear conscience. Field savvy should involve not just methods of gathering facts but common sense and accumulated experience as well. This nurtures concern, responsibility, and restraint, which, in turn, yield effectiveness. Technique is extremely important.

When we climbed past the tiercel's sentinel rock, his anxious—but not panicked—mate slid slowly off to the west and began her ringing soar, watching the happenings at her nest as she rose.

FEMALE LARK BUNTING

THREE-WEEK-OLD EAGLET

Like the Foundation Eyrie, the Indian Eyrie could almost be reached without ropes. A two-foot-wide ledge just below the cliff top—on the side away from the prairie falcon wintering ledge—led to within one good-sized leap of the eaglets. Although the nest could have held both Jack and me at the same time, we never chanced the jump; the dangers presented by the forty-five-foot drop-off, a rock overhang that sheltered the nest, and similar logistical problems expected during the return jump to the ledge were too great. Later, when we placed leg bands on the birds, ropes would be needed.

From six feet away, I could see that all was not well in the eyrie.

"One of the birds is half again as big as the other," I shouted up to Jack, who was standing directly above me, "and they're fighting like crazy!"

"Must be a Cain and Abel battle," Jack said. "How serious is it?"

"I can't tell. Come take a look."

As near as we could determine, the larger bird—Old Witch, we came to call her—had hatched about April 21st, at least two or three days before Abel, the smaller one. It is not clear how such inequities in hatching times develop or if one bird just grows more slowly after hatching. However, if incubation starts with the first egg deposited, that egg hatches earlier, and fratricide may result if the discrepancy is large. Fortunately, such circumstances are not as characteristic of golden eagles as of some closely related European and African eagles; for example, the black or Verreaux's eagle. Two young are rarely, if ever, reared in the same black eagle nest; the stronger kills its nestmate or pushes it overboard.

There was a vast difference in the stage of development of the two eaglets in the Indian Eyrie. Only Old Witch showed visible flight-feather development; her pinfeathers were just beginning to open and show through the down. At just over three weeks of age, both birds were almost resistant to cold—not in need of brooding except at night and during inclement weather. During an eagle's third and fourth weeks, the thicker, second covering of down emerges, mostly from new feather follicles. The first down is later pushed out at the tips of flight and body feathers, and it finally flakes away. New down feathers bloom like flowers, forming a soft cotton-like covering over an inch thick in places. I could readily see both types of down feathers on the eaglets, particularly on the head of the female where hair-like bristles of natal down stood higher than the barely fluffed second covering.

Abel's lower back was severely scarred. Each time he gave in to the bullying of his sibling, he turned his back on her; but she continued to peck and tear at him, and he twittered in pain. He was also soiled from trying to escape her advances, but he seemed otherwise alert and healthy.

"Think we should go get the climbing gear and get him out of there?" I asked Jack.

"You're the boss," he answered.

"Thanks, Jake."

"There might be more to learn by leaving him there," Jack added.

Knowing that nest failure or nestling death is likely, one finds it difficult sometimes not to take over from nature. Runts like Abel are good candidates for hand care, as are birds at nest sites that fail year after year. Many times I had to bite my lip to turn away and leave eggs or eyases where failure was imminent. It was not always easy to define a "clear conscience" when leaving such a nest, because there is a little of Saint Francis of Assisi in all of us—a little pity for troubled animals.

My sympathies were with Abel, but we decided to leave him in the ring for a few more rounds and to check on him as often as possible.

Pity was unnecessary at the Cottonwood Eyrie, our last stop on May 14th to check on nesting eagles. Through the weeks, the female parent had become so habituated to seeing the rancher—and occasionally Jack and me—that she rarely showed signs of alarm as long as we stayed near the windmill, two hundred yards away. That day she showed no fear at all during our visit.

"Looks like summer might come after all," I said to Jack as we walked away from the windmill toward the nest. "This is the first shirtsleeve weather we've had."

"I can wait," he said. "The next time we walk over here and back, the water at that windmill will look pretty good; and it'll look better every time as it gets hotter. I'll remind you someday by diving into one of those tanks."

Each windmill pumps only a small stream of water out of the ground, which is then piped a few feet by gravity flow into one or more open aboveground storage tanks. The tanks, like some portable swimming pools, are just the right height for a cow to reach in and suck several gallons of water into its four stomachs.

"You can have it," I said. "There's too much gunk on the bottom of those tanks, like cow manure and dead birds."

Quite a few birds, including some young eagles, fall into the tanks and drown trying to drink or to bathe, and cows have to dip their dirty faces into the water each time they drink. We always tried to find a tiny piece of board to float in each tank, something that smaller birds could climb onto to keep from drowning; but there was little we could do about the cows' dirt.

"Besides," I continued, "we won't be checking nests when it's a hundred in the shade. That's a good way to kill eyases."

Heat prostration of young raptors has probably been noted in western North American golden eagles more than in any other region or raptorial species, although it is not a common occurrence. Nevertheless, disturbing nests after lunchtime on days when the temperature is ninety degrees or more is not worth the risk. One can never leave an unshaded nest with a clear conscience in such circumstances.

"Hey, she's sitting pretty tight today," I said as we got to within a hundred feet of her. "She really is calm about the whole thing, just like when I tried to stare her down two weeks ago."

"She's not sitting, she's standing; but look at the way she's doing it," Jack said as he handed me the scope. "She's got her head down and her body pressed tight against a branch behind her. And her eyes are half shut. She's hiding from us."

"I think you're right. Have you ever seen that before?" I asked.

"Never," Jack said.

"You know, if I hadn't known she was there, I might not have seen the outline of an eagle."

"Yes, but you would have seen how dark she is compared to the sticks of the nest," Jack said. "You can see that a half-mile away with the scope, even when they're lying flat."

"I don't mean she would have gotten by us; but we wouldn't kill her either. That must help conceal her from all the city folk running around loose out here, though."

We walked closer and stopped about thirty feet from the tree. She held her position as if she had died standing up.

"Maybe she's dead, Jake," I said.

"Not a chance. She knows what's going on. You stay here and talk to her and I'll walk around the tree. Tell her we won't be here long," he suggested jokingly.

"Hey, sweetheart," I said to the eagle. "It's time for you to split. You've been found and we want to get out of here and leave you alone, but first we're going to see how you're treating your kids."

She did not move a feather.

"Hell, what can you say to an eagle when she refuses to answer?" I called to Jack. Then I gave a loud, wailing whistle, but it did not faze her.

Jack slapped the tree lightly a couple of times only twenty-five feet below her and commanded in a firm voice, "Come on, eagle. Don't be stupid. Straighten up and fly right."

We had never before seen such behavior.

"This damned bird is part mule," Jack said. "What's she so proud of?"

He walked off about forty feet on the other side of the tree for another look. We had her surrounded, but she held her ground. It must have been a sight: two grown men standing below a tree waving their arms and jumping up and down, as if trying to flag a fast freight. Maybe golden eagles are aloof and not timid, I thought; but that bird was an exception.

As Jack walked back toward me, the largest golden eagle I had ever seen—or so it seemed at the time—straightened up, took two slow steps to the nest rim, and fell nonchalantly into the air. She had to drop a few feet to avoid the thick crown of the tree, but she soon started her ascent to get overhead.

"I'll bet her young are less than two days old," I said as I climbed onto Jack's shoulders to reach the first limb.

"If they are, they're getting a late start," he grunted.

Live cottonwoods are easy to climb, as long as one is careful to avoid dead limbs and loose bark. I was soon sitting astride a large limb looking down at a thirteen- or fourteen-day-old eaglet—the same age as those in the Foundation Eyrie. A large food cache testified to the youngster's opulent comfort.

Its breadwinning father and protective mother were certainly the

SHORT-HORNED LIZARD

most dutiful eagles we ever found. Both wheeled above us, as they should have been doing all along, while we later sipped fresh cool water back at the windmill. Not from the tank: it is better to intercept a drink at the end of the outlet pipe!

Following the check of eagles on May 14th, the weather turned calm and dry for a week, an unwelcome sunning for the wizened prairie—and for the farmers whose concern for their dry-land crops was growing. Jack and I visited the Foundation, Indian, and Cottonwood Eyries on May 19th; all was well. At four weeks of age, the eaglets at the Indian Eyrie were still feuding, but Abel seemed to be withstanding Old Witch's attacks, even though he was a full week behind her in development. Her second down was in full bloom, and the tips of her major wing feathers showed as a string of black beads draped across each of her snow-white sides. The smaller bird's down feathers were still mostly his first set; the pins of his major feathers remained below the fluff.

The Oil Well Eyrie eagles had been spending their time at two windmills north of the oil well, as distant from the Foundation Eyrie as possible without meeting opposition from nesting eagles farther north. The spirit of courtship that I saw above the Oil Well Eyrie in late March of 1971 was a far cry from the sulks caused by the premature end of parental responsibility in those eagles' lives.

Jack and I also put the agreeable weather to good use studying the other raptors. In the majority of groves we checked, we saw Swainson's hawks building nests. Most great horned owls fledged in mid-May. Only ferruginous hawks and prairie falcons were in the holding pattern of incubation, but that was soon to change.

In fact, the nesting seasons of all species were in such full swing in late May that Jack and I could not keep up with our priority assignment, the thousand-square-mile area, let alone visit the obvious nests on the adjacent thousand square miles. Even the late incubation period of Swainson's hawks did not provide a respite, because their tardiness required double and triple checking of every tree. It was the busiest time— by far!—for nest searching; we had no time for interruptions like bad weather.

Thus Jack and I left town on May 21st in spite of a strong wind. Traffic lights swung heavily in warm breezes gusting to thirty-five miles an hour, and small highway signs twisted back and forth below a clear sky. A few scattered thunderstorms had passed during the night ahead of a rapidly approaching low-pressure center from the Gulf of Mexico, the kind that generates tornadoes when it meets cool northern air. The southeasterly wind told us that the violent weather was still south of us. Yet, when we passed a stretch of highway that crossed several hundred acres of barren sand dunes, the whole world seemed to be heading southeast; for a few moments, at least, the dust-bowl days had returned.

"We're not going to be able to do much today," I said to Jack as he sped blindly through the small sandstorm.

"Let's do a roadside count!" he said facetiously, knowing that nearly all raptors would be out of sight—sitting on nests, lying on the ground, or perching in the lees of cliffs, trees, or bushes.

"Why not?" I said. "Better yet, let's go count smashed Swainson's hawk eggs."

We both knew that I was not joking about the eggs. Most Swainson's hawks had partial clutches in their flimsy nests: the wind was increasing; and a dark storm cloud looming on the southern horizon seemed to be coming our way.

The conversation continued in a pessimistic vein.

"I don't mind losing a few Swainson's hawks," Jack said. "They breed like rats anyway. But if this gets much worse, there'll be dead ferrugs, too, and that's not cool."

Jack always had his favorites. The ferruginous hawk was just spectacular enough to win his favor—mine, too, for that matter, although I tried harder not to look down my nose at the other species.

"Let's go check the Swainson's hawks along Sand Creek to see how they're taking it," I suggested. "I'd like to see how they ride it out."

"Or don't ride it out!" Jack said, stating the obvious.

In less than ten minutes, we were parked two hundred feet from a grove of tall cottonwoods that stood single file along a dry stream bed about thirty miles west of the Eagle Breaks—closer to home.

"Wasn't the nest in the third tree from the end?" I asked, without a nest in sight.

"It was," Jack answered, "but you'd never know it now."

To confirm our fears, we walked over to the tree in the vandalish winds. Sand and dust were swept from the creek bed into my squinted eyes and between my teeth. I halfheartedly tried to run down a tumble-weed; it beat me at twenty yards, but was snatched still as a statue by a barbed-wire fence just seconds later.

The frivolity did not change the outcome of our trek.

"Here's an egg—or what's left of it," Jack called above the rustle of half-open leaves.

He was standing about thirty feet downwind of the nest tree, holding several yolk-stained eggshell fragments.

"The whole nest must have lifted off at once to throw it that far," I called back while looking around for a nest we never found.

"Well, that's how they ride out a good wind," Jack said, tongue in cheek, as we headed back to the truck.

He knew that I was disappointed; I do not see yolk from hawk eggs and chicken eggs with the same eyes.

The spasms of the wind-shaken trees left little wonder about why some hawk nests tip or blow out completely. When we arrived at another nest a mile downstream from the first, the female was hanging on for dear lives—the lives she was assigned to incubate and later to nurture during several acts of summer's play. It was important for her to stay on her nest during the windstorm because her two and a half pounds helped to hold the nest in place.

"She's hangin' in there, Jake," I said excitedly, one eye fixed to the scope. "She's facing directly into the wind and lying just as low as she can. That's incredible! The limb must be swinging two or three feet each way."

"She'll make it okay," Jack predicted. "Her nest is closer to the tree trunk than the other one."

"That's the only thing that'll save her," I said. "I wonder if she's gripping the nest with her feet. That could be why we don't lose very many older nestlings to the wind; they're heavier, and they can grip the nest just like adults. It's eggs and helpless downies that get it."

As the first pelts of raindrops began sounding on the truck roof, Jack suggested we move on.

"We'll get dumped on if we stay here much longer," he said, pointing to a nearly cloud-filled southern sky. "That cloud's coming from the wrong direction."

He was right. It was much more difficult to dodge storms that slipped north along the east slope of the Rockies than to avoid thunderheads that formed over the mountains and then moved east.

"Think we should call it a day?" I asked, half hoping that he would agree. "It looks pretty widespread, and the weatherman wasn't too encouraging."

"Neither is the weather!" Jack added hastily. "But our wives might faint if we got home before noon."

"Yes, but my kids won't," I said. "Besides, it's Sunday."

That settled it. The forty-mile drive back home took about fifty minutes, ten more than usual because of the headwind and two brief hailstorms that pelted the ground with marbles of ice. I hoped that the hawks would weather the hail better than the horned larks and other small ground-nesting dickey birds.

13

A SOLID
EXPERIENCE

For a week, beginning June 3rd, Jack and I had with us one of only two visitors we invited out that summer. We did not run anything approaching a guide service, even for friends, because of the amount of work to be done and the large responsibility we felt for the birds' secrecy. But Giles Greenfield had come to the States from England only the year before, and at a raptor conference Jack and I attended the Englishman had casually sold himself to us as a conscientious raptor type. To wheedle—as I now accuse him—an invitation to the study area, he used the same slow-talking super-polite technique on me that he used in selling machinery, which was his job, for a large Indiana industrial firm. I did not know that he was not satisfied with his work until he wrote in the spring of 1972:

> Butch, my reason for writing is to ask you for advice. I
> have decided to leave industry, where I have been for the last
> eleven years, and to start doing something that *I* want to do.

Giles had developed a yearning, stronger than most people's, to do his own thing; he was also searching for a little adventure with raptors. The experience he found was so mind-boggling that he and his wife returned a month later—to live!

Early in his life, Giles, like Jack and me, had not been kindled by any of the urban recreations. Ours are more venerable pastimes: canoeing peaceful rivers in the solitude of being carried along in body and spirit by the forces of nature; hiking through woods or across open country—tundra, prairies, or moors—to see wild things where they live; and tramping the field to run a rabbit for a trained goshawk—delights that develop step by step, month after long month, all for a few fleet chases and even fewer quarry. Compare the long-awaited jackrabbit kill by a goshawk, using only nature's primitive rules, to six points scored for running a football across a line drawn by man during a game of his own recent rule-making; compare the evening songfest of the prairie to the uproar of a home run during a twi-night doubleheader; or compare the gentle sounds of canoe paddles stirring a slow-moving stream to the racket of stricken bowling pins.

Alas! The urban amusements are no less satisfying to their participants and fans; it is just that our obsessions are set afire by different activities.

As we motored, as Giles would say—not drove—toward the Eagle Breaks early that morning, we showed him a number of hawk nests and told each one's story as we passed it.

"This is Bull Corner," I said, pointing out three huge Hereford bulls that ruled the pasture. "Swainson's hawks have nested in that cottonwood tree for the past three years, and horned owls usually nest over there in that Chinese elm."

Neither site was more than fifty feet off the road.

Less than a hundred yards farther, I added, "And ferruginous hawks fledged two young from the nest in that big tree. As we walked in to band them one year, the adult female dropped a thirteen-lined ground squirrel at my feet. That happens, occasionally, and I wonder sometimes if they'd do the same to a coyote to distract it. A coyote couldn't get young out of *that* nest, but a lot of ferrugs nest flat on the ground. It'd be like me throwing a beefsteak to a grizzly to save my kids."

"What's that you're writing?" Jack asked, seeing Giles scribbling in his notebook.

"I must make a record of all the hawks I see," Giles answered optimistically.

"Did you hear that, Doc?" Jack bellowed. "He's going to write down every bird of prey we see!"

We smiled, knowing that such a task was sheer folly; he would have to work hard just to get the number and species.

After motoring another twenty miles along an improved dirt road, we came to pavement again.

"Well, that's it," I said facetiously, expecting a shoulder shrug, no more, as approval. "You've seen it all."

"Great!" Giles answered, with wide-eyed wonderment. "Let's go find some new nests. Is there anything in those trees ahead? Didn't you say that you had some eagle and prairie falcon nests?"

"Oh, yeah, but we don't show those to just anybody," Jack said, with a straight face.

Giles accepted that matter-of-factly. He certainly would not have shown a hawk nest to just anybody—an unwritten rule among raptor people.

Jack looked at me as if to say: "Boy, is he ever in for a surprise!" How could he get so stimulated about driving past a few horned owl, Swainson's hawk, and ferruginous hawk nests? I thought. The problem was that Jack and I had never been to Indiana or England, where, by comparison, one finds only a sprinkling of spectacular nesting raptors.

Soon we came to the trees that Giles was curious about.

"I don't know about those, but I guess we could check them," I said. "Have you ever walked them, Jack?"

"No."

We had, of course, many times; and we knew that there was a nest near the far end of the grove.

"Is there ever any water in this creek?" Giles asked as I spread the barbed-wire fence at the side of the road for him.

He waved me through and then nonchalantly stepped over the top strand, his lean six-foot-four frame aiding his maneuver.

"Yeah, it runs about one month each year—usually May—unless we get a big storm," Jack answered.

We walked about a hundred yards, passed the nest, and then the trees petered out.

"Doesn't look promising," I lamented, still pulling his leg.

As we came back to the largest cottonwood, I stopped, looked at Giles, and asked, "Well, are you going to climb it or not, Giles?"

"Climb what?"

"This tree, to see what's in that nest up there," I said, turning his shoulders and pointing to where he should look. "Check twenty feet up, in that crotch."

In Giles's defense, I must say that the leaves were quite thick; but our visitor had failed to see all the whitewash on the ground when we had walked past the tree before.

I found out much later that Giles is deathly afraid of heights; ten feet above the ground might as well be a thousand. He still talks about the mental adjustment he had to make to cope with the stepladder of large limbs up to that nest.

Giles began his ascent, shaking with excitement and phobia. He continued on up in spite of thick mutes on the branches, and the odor and flies from rotten meat scraps. Until he looked over the edge of the nest, he had no idea that he had climbed to a golden eagle eyrie!

There she was, at about forty-nine days, the oldest eaglet on the study area. The surprise did not spur Giles's confidence: her wings were open, the tips helping her to stand tall; her head was held high, neck ballooned by the erection of new feathers; her mouth was open, beak ready to snip; and she leaned back a little to lead with her oversized feet poised for grabbing. The bird was all aggression with a man so close.

Giles talked to the eagle in an unsteady but understanding tone, unable to tame a single feather. As he moved to ready his camera, she lurched forward, grabbed with her feet, hissed through her wide-open mouth, and swatted the nest with her wings for balance—all in one menacing action. Giles nearly bailed out of the tree, but fought his fears until he had clicked half a roll of pictures. Before we left, we counted seventeen hind feet of cottontails and jackrabbits, all collected since our last visit three weeks before.

In five minutes we were motoring still farther east.

"Where were the adult eagles?" Giles asked.

"They were probably high overhead, but I never saw them," Jack answered. "You'd have a tough time seeing an adult in a nest with a seven-week-old eaglet. They don't want to get into a nest with a crazy eyas any more than you do. So they usually just drop food and split."

"That was a great surprise, you know, because the only eagle eyries I've ever seen were in Scotland, on very bleak, remote, inaccessible granite cliffs, where there was no such thing as a 'walk-in' situation," Giles explained. "It never entered my mind that there could possibly be an eagle nesting fifteen or twenty feet above the ground in a tree—and only two hundred bloody feet from a paved highway as well."

What had become almost an everyday occurrence to Jack and me had made a profound impression on Giles; we were beginning to understand the limits of his previous experience in other parts of the world.

"Check that bird, Giles," Jack said as we arrived at Raven Tree a trifle before eight that morning.

Raven Tree was the first scheduled stop on our spectacular itinerary, which also included banding the eaglets in the Foundation, Indian, and Cottonwood Eyries, and climbing to the Breaks Falcon Eyrie. The female ferruginous hawk stood tall in the Raven Tree nest, but she flew off as soon as Giles threw the truck door open, jumped out, and trained his binoculars on her, practically all in one movement and almost before we stopped rolling.

"Look at that gorgeous creature, would you?" Giles said slowly, with obvious appreciation.

Jack and I, compelled by our excitement, always flaunted the sweet guilt of being on the grasslands studying raptors full time; nothing did us more good than showing an appreciative visitor a few young eagles, prairie falcons, and ferruginous hawks. But it was not selfish gloating; we wanted more to share our collective experiences with someone who would savor them, just as I had looked forward to April 1st, when Jack joined me, so that I could share my observations with him.

"You'll never guess, Giles, how I positively identified my first ferruginous hawk," I said as the three of us walked to the Chinese elm tree.

"You shot it!" Jack interjected in total jest.

"Right," I sang out, looking at Giles to see if he detected the false air.

Apparently he did not; he looked condescendingly down his nose at us, his eyes wider than open.

"You *what*?" he cried.

"Shucks, Giles, you know I wouldn't do that," I drawled. "Actually, I was at a nest, the bird soared up, and then it screamed just like that one."

I pointed to the plaintful bird gaining altitude just north of us, and continued, "If you'll check the size of its mouth each time it screams, you'll know it's a ferrug."

Giles then sensed a put-on, yet the statement was straight. When I first walked the grasslands in 1967, I identified all ferruginous hawks as light-phase red-tailed hawks, a perfectly natural mistake, I suppose. I corrected myself the next spring after observing a big-mouthed ferruginous hawk screaming above a nest.

But picture poor Giles walking beside two near strangers, one a super-straight Ph.D. possessed by a penchant for lighthearted sarcasm, and the other an indiscreet, self-styled pugilist easily set off by sarcasm for any reason. A third person might—though wrongly—conclude that Jack and I have no mutual respect whatsoever as we debate back and forth, mostly about raptors, each with a very different style. We did not pull our verbal punches just because we had a visitor along.

To Giles—poor chap—the impulsive changes from battles royal to friendly frivolities between Jack and me were a source of immediate confusion; he was someone new I could take a rap at and someone Jack could chop logic with, all while a refined British temperament under-went a hot-air treatment, from both his verbose hosts and the weather. Jack and I brought up the old battles—roadside counts, "those damned numbers," and the need for a large study area—and we expected Giles to be an impartial and knowledgeable one-man jury.

As Giles climbed Raven Tree, I recalled taking one of my nephews, Tom, Jr., to a ferruginous hawk nest on his first day out the year before. Tom, a thirteen-year-old Alaskan, was so anxious to see some young hawks that he climbed the wrong tree. Without looking, he struggled upward about fifteen feet with much more difficulty that it would have taken to shin up the nest tree. Finally, he glanced overhead, down to me, and then across to the nest ten feet away. He nearly fell as he slapped his forehead, embarrassed and dismayed. Giles, the elder by nearly two decades, managed to climb the right tree—but then there were no other trees within three miles of Raven Tree.

"If I aged those birds right on our last visit, the oldest ones should have a good start on their second down, especially on the antebrachium," I predicted pompously.

"What's that?" Giles asked, politely disgusted with my technical jargon.

"Forearm," I called back. "Don't birds have forearms in England?"

"Why didn't you say forearm in the first place?" he responded, again with that condescending look.

"How's the smallest bird?" I asked. "Tail End Charlie, we call him."

"He's too small, dirty as sin, and the other birds are sitting on the grubby thing," Giles answered. "And the others have food in their crops; he's starving."

Jack and I had checked Raven Tree for the first time on May 28th, and had found a moderately staggered hatch; the young were apparently one, two, four, and four days old. Yet by June 3rd Charlie was only half the size of his largest nestmates: about five ounces instead of ten and about five or six days behind in development. He was much like Abel, the smaller eaglet in the Indian Eyrie, although Tail End Charlie was not being attacked by his brothers and sisters. His problem was his own inability to compete for food.

Parent raptors generally cater to whichever mouth is open the widest and thrust the highest; thus runts are frequently neglected until all others are satisfied. But young ferruginous hawks, like most other raptors, are generally fed small prey at first: fledgling horned larks and young thirteen-lined ground squirrels, for examples. At ten days of age, an eyas ferruginous hawk can eat most or all of one small animal at each meal; the parents must bring three or four prey in rapid succession before a runt in a brood of four or five gets fed. By that time, the first strong bird may be ready to eat again, and it quite naturally consumes the runt's portion. Accordingly, we found more runts in large broods of ferruginous hawks than among nestlings of other species.

Young golden eagles are treated differently. From the start they are fed from larger animals—cottontails, jackrabbits, and pheasants. The strongest nestling can be satisfied before an entire prey item is consumed. Thus, if a Cain and Abel feud is not carried to fatality, the cheated bird will still get fed. We were optimistic about the future of Abel, but Tail End Charlie was another matter.

Giles held one of the older eyases up, so that I could confirm its age from the ground. I had been close enough: give or take a day, ten days old. Charlie's nestmates were well into their periods of rapid weight gain, ballooning at about two ounces each day.

"How about prey items?" I asked, trying to get all necessary information without climbing to the nest myself.

"None that I can see," Giles answered.

Charlie's plight foretold that.

"Well, let's go, then," I said quickly. "We've got a lot of work to do."

Giles looked at me, head cocked and puzzled. Was he questioning calling our activities work? Did he want to stay longer?

Then he glanced at Tail End Charlie. "Poor fellow! You are not going to leave him here, are you?" he asked, full of concern and indignation.

"For now, at least," I answered.

Giles's retreat from the tree was slow. Then I told him about the next planned stop—the prairie falcon eyrie—to take his mind off Charlie's uncertain fate; but it did not work. We drove east toward Cattle Pond while the three of us discussed Giles's first ferruginous hawk nest.

"I cannot imagine why any hawk would build such a huge nest in such a stupid small tree," Giles noted, shaking his head in amazement.

Jack briefly explained the history of the nest site: homesteading, cattle ranching, and the threat of cultivation. I mentioned the major types of ferruginous hawk nest sites: on the ground—a creek bank, low cliff, isolated outcrop, or the crest of a gentle hill; low in a short, usually introduced tree, like the Chinese elm at Raven Tree; or high in a tall cottonwood along a creek bottom.

"If ferruginous hawks nest anywhere near cultivation, the nest is usually high in a cottonwood," I explained, "but in cattle country all three situations are used."

"Butch, what are you going to do with Tail End Charlie?" Giles asked, apparently thinking more of the bird than of the natural-history lessons it had taken years for Jack and me to learn.

I tried to put Giles's mind to rest with the pendulum-of-nature idea, with the thought that saving every eyas is not important to population dynamics, and with the idea that biting one's lip is part of being a naturalist. He listened, but his nods were less than straight up and down.

I suppose I was more optimistic about Charlie's fate because of things I had learned during my doctoral research on hawk growth. After hatching several ferruginous, red-tailed, and Swainson's hawk eggs in an incubator, a rare and touching occupation back in my graduate school days, I dutifully reared the little beggars from size 1 to full growth, weighing them daily and measuring eighteen different body parts at least once a week. I smothered myself with data on the development of legs, toes, claws, wings, beaks, and feathers.

In addition, I kept records of food consumption during each of their five daily meals. These were the data that lessened the urgency of Charlie's plight. During the first year of my laboratory research, I found that a female ferruginous hawk required about five and a half times as many ounces of food as she gained in weight between hatching and fledging. The next year, for reasons I still puzzle over, it took only three and a half times as much food (about a third less) to rear a similar bird to the *same* top weight.

Regardless of the cause of these differences—perhaps it was dissimilar food quality, hatching technique, or rearing technique—the mere potential for that much variation in food requirements implies that young birds in broods of three or four can attain adult proportions on a greatly reduced food supply, if necessary, without eliminating one or two nestlings to decrease the energy requirement of the entire brood. This would lead to a higher nesting success during poor prey years than would be possible if food consumption was not potentially variable.

Even in Charlie's case, although he might have taken a week longer to reach top weight, as happened in the laboratory, he might still have made it eventually.

"Hey, Jake, it looks like the Swainson's hawks at Cattle Pond are going to lay again," I said as we stopped briefly on the road near the lone cottonwood.

Giles had never seen a Swainson's hawk nest close up, either; he was temporarily drawn away from Charlie's plight upon seeing a western kingbird vigorously harassing the hawk perched on a completely rebuilt nest.

"We had a bad windstorm on May 21st," Jack explained to Giles, "and the first nest was blown out of that tree. These birds should lay a second clutch soon. It usually takes fourteen to sixteen days for them to recycle and lay again."

The May windstorm had, in fact, set the pattern of Swainson's hawk egg-laying. Those that laid after the wind—as at Honey Locust Shack—stayed with their first clutches. Of those Swainson's hawks that laid before May 21st, about one pair out of ten lost their eggs; as a result, a second, smaller peak of egg production came about June 6th.

There was a definite air of this new potential at Cattle Pond: a rebuilt nest and the normal, almost incessant harassment of the hawks by kingbirds. Like many late-arriving migratory birds, kingbirds depend heavily on mosquitoes, mayflies, gnats, flying ants, and a myriad of other airborne insects for food. These large flycatchers nest wherever at least one good-sized tree grows, even if there is a hawk nest in it! The precious shade of trees attracts cattle, and the livestock bring insects with them—a dandy state of affairs for kingbirds, though not for hawks.

As we watched the action at Cattle Pond, the other hawk flew in and was intercepted by the kingbird.

"Look at that bloody devil attack, would you?" Giles said excitedly.

"Watch and you'll see *Tyrannus verticalis* take a short ride," I said.

Giles did a double take at hearing the kingbird's scientific name, but resumed watching the one-sided tormenting.

Swainson's hawks seem to exist for the sheer delight of kingbirds. The little pest finally grasped the hawk's nape and rode on top of its head for forty feet or more, pulled along like a kite on a short string; but the hawk, accustomed to such frequent trespasses, barely broke from its path to a limb near its mate.

Along the road north to the Breaks, we encountered another late-arriving insectivorous bird, a common nighthawk, sleeping on a fence post. These non-raptorial birds are closely related to the whippoorwill and are attracted to places like Cattle Pond and Antelope Reservoir by flying insects that live their larval stages in water. The milling birds greatly animate summer sunsets, both visually and audibly: long narrow wings float their robin-sized bodies gracefully over the well-ventilated prairie: their eerie sounds fill the countryside with buzzing calls and whiz-booms caused by sudden pullouts from nose dives. A thousand echoes of crickets, as many hoarse tones of spadefoot toads, occasional howls of coyotes and hoots of owls, and the familiar singsongs of meadowlarks add volume and variety to evening songfests on the shortgrass prairie.

Before we stopped below the Breaks Falcon Eyrie, I had got the equipment ready for banding the eyas falcons. Scientists band birds to learn about their seasonal movements and their longevity. Each metal ring has stamped on it an address and an eight-digit number, different for each bird. Unfortunately, most band recoveries mean that the birds have died. For example, 599-03923 was a golden eagle banded as a nestling near the Eagle Breaks in June of 1971 and found dead the following January ninety-two miles east. As suggested by that and other band returns, immature golden eagles fledged near the Breaks do not move very far south in the winter.

On the other hand, if that January someone recovered band number 727-01534, one put on a Swainson's hawk the preceding July, the person and the hawk would most likely have been in Argentina, the wintering grounds of Swainson's hawks.

Following tiercel prairie falcon number 686-00135 to get a band return every month after it was banded at the Eagle Breaks in 1971 would probably have led several hundred miles north or northeast of the Breaks—even as far north as the prairie provinces of Canada—from July through October. Prairie falcons move north after fledging, but during the winter months, those banded as nestlings just east of the Rockies tend to move progressively south through the Dakotas, Nebraska, and Kansas, perhaps even into Oklahoma and as far east as Missouri and Iowa. But one bird cannot be followed continuously, so banders use individual returns collected over a number of years to map movements in detail.

Before leaving the truck for the prairie falcon eyrie, Jack loaded his shoulders with his camera and the climbing gear: a hundred and fifty

BULL SNAKE

feet of nylon rope; a nylon strap as wide as but longer than a belt, which is used to form a cradle or seat for the climber; and two carabiners with brake bars—small oblong metal rings through which the rope is threaded to slow the climber's descent. In his hands Jack carried the scope and a crash helmet used when rappelling on loose rock. A cold-cocked climber is too soon a dead one! I carried a tackle box full of metal bands, pliers, and banding sheets; a notebook and pen to record general information; an old camera bag and a ball of nylon string to transport the eyases to the top of the cliff; and a triple-beam balance with which to weigh them. Giles carried only his camera, his binoculars, and himself across a quarter-mile of prairie and up a short rock chimney that led to the cliff top.

He must have snapped two dozen pictures along the way—everything from clouds to a bull snake we found crossing a small dry wash. On top of the cliff he was nearly as busy.

"Where is this prairie falcon you keep telling me about?" he bantered impatiently, implying that we were not producing enough birds for him.

He was beginning to understand the hot-and-cold-running comradeship that kept Jack and me alert; it was a short rocky road to the heart of the matter.

"She's there, just over the edge of the cliff," I assured Giles, but then added, "I think."

Even I get apprehensive when not given a "keck-keck-keck" welcome.

"She's still proud of her kids, so she'll stay put until I throw the rope over," Jack announced confidently as he prepared the rope and climbing gear.

We kept talking aloud to let the falcon know where we were. Giles glassed the prairie—all forty or so miles of it in every direction except north, where the ridge between the Breaks and the Oil Well Eyrie-Battle Gap creek bed intervened. It was a beautiful vista and such a nice day; there was so little to see, yet there was so much.

"Cattle Pond is there—south of us, a little over three miles," I told Giles. "Just to the right is Raven Tree and Tail End Charlie. Due west of us is what we call Honey Locust Shack, where Swainson's hawks have nested for the past two years."

I began searching for a large rock, a yucca plant, or a lump of rabbitbrush to brace my heels against; it was my job to hold the rope for Jack. I thought for a moment, called Giles over to my chosen rock, and sat *him* down behind it.

"Get comfortable," I directed, "and make some nice heel holes that won't bust out with two hundred and six pounds pulling on your hips."

"You're not serious—are you?" he said, ending with a gaping jaw that did not rise to the occasion.

"Why not? You've got to earn your keep somehow."

Giles had little idea what would be expected of him, but there were no trees to tie the rope to; someone had to hold the other end of Jack's lifeline.

"Are you sure you want to do it this way, Jack?" Giles said.

"Not unless you want me to hold—and you rappel!" Jack said as he slung the nylon strap around his rear, gathered a loop on each side and another through his crotch, and then snapped all three loops into one carabiner close to his belly.

Again we got that wide-eyed look of doubt down Giles's nose; but he did not say another word.

"Gee, I'm glad you're here," I said, wrapping the rope four times around the Englishman's hips. "Now take the short end and wrap it around the business rope several times. That makes a better handhold, and it guarantees Jack that you'll scrape and scratch to stop yourself from being dragged over the cliff in case everything breaks loose and you drop him. He just wants to know that you'll be working hard for him in case he's killed."

Giles was perplexed in trying to determine if my reasons were real or another put-on; he was uneasy about the unfamiliar responsibility.

"It's not hard," Jack reassured him. "There'll be quite a tug; that's all. Can you imagine doing this all alone by just tying onto that rock? I used to do it that way, but, hell, there's places out here where they'd never find the body if you fell. I'm always happier knowing that someone will at least know where my body is. I don't know why, I just am."

Giles produced another grim-faced nod. He was not comforted one bit, even though the most difficult job was Jack's—by his own choosing, of course; the climber gets to see everything firsthand.

Jack coiled the rope carefully, flung it over the cliff, and checked to be sure that the end reached the ground. That flushed the falcon.

"Howdy, honey!" he shouted as she flew south a hundred yards and then returned, "kecking" and climbing continually.

I sat down as soon as the bird flew, hoping that she would attack more vigorously and spectacularly if she was not intimidated so much by my presence. I would expect the same cheap favor from Jack if I was kneeling at the edge of the cliff with my back to an aggressive bird, unless that bird was the more dangerous great horned owl.

The falcon swooped past about six feet from Jack's helmeted head on her first in run.

"Sock it to him!" I urged, glancing at Giles.

He was still speechless, but his eyes, as big as saucers and not at all condescending, told the whole story of his deliverance. For that moment, at least, he was doing his own thing! He had found his little adventure with raptors.

I am compelled at this point to contradict two old-wives' tales that keep surfacing in the arguments of people who criticize, on purely emotional grounds, the type of activity I am describing. First of all, if young birds are touched by man, their parents will not abandon them; I have years of data and volumes of literature that prove my point. Secondly, it is myth that parent birds show great anguish at being disturbed on their nests—even at having one or two of several young removed or destroyed naturally or unnaturally. I do not see anguish in either the aggressive intruder reaction of prairie falcons or the timid but watchful soaring of golden eagles.

On the other hand, destruction of all eggs or nestlings in a nest can produce behaviors that man may well interpret as the sulks—as I did in the Oil Well Eyrie eagles after their eggs were destroyed. Even that analysis is probably wrought with too much reading of my own feelings into the situation; but it is not as absurd as the emotional argument that birds should not be studied because interference unnerves them. Anyone who has ever been struck by a horned owl or a prairie falcon knows that they are not unglued from their purpose; theirs is mostly instinctive business, not the result of derangement of some mental process through some equally unreal capacity to smell the touch of man or to count nestlings after a naturalist's visit. The problems of visiting nests are both practical and solvable; they are *not* emotional on the bird's part.

Wildlife needs empathy rooted in experience and technical understanding more than sympathy grown in ignorance and fertilized with emotion—and that applies from extreme to extreme, from eagle-killing sheep ranchers to radical conservationists.

I doubt that Giles even felt the rope pull as Jack eased over the precipice and freed his fingers, which at first were always smashed between the cliff and the rope. The knuckle-scraping technique allows him to go over slowly and to keep from dislodging rocks that might injure young birds. Then the climber leaned back to position his legs between himself and the cliff. Once he was in this very unnatural stance—legs perpendicular to the cliff, leaning back on sixty vertical feet of air, more or less suspended by a rope tied at his navel—Jack's initial muscle work was finished. He was standing on the nest ledge after two short hops, simultaneously paying out the rope through his right hand, around his waist, and through the carabiners.

The falcon continued her attacks with undaunted spirit. In the distance, out over the grass, I saw and heard the tiercel, and I pointed out the timid fellow to Giles. Shyness is typical of male prairie falcons.

Then the rope slackened, and Jack whistled.

"You can get up now," I told Giles.

A whistle meant that Jack was secure on the ledge; nevertheless, Giles chose to tend the rope until he was safely on the ground. I lowered the camera bag and Jack filled it with two fifteen-day-old prairie falcons, which I promptly raised to the top of the cliff. Then I carried them to Giles's position. After taking each one out and examining it, I placed it between Giles's legs. Three more falcons came up in two more bagloads.

"Let's see, males take size 6, and females take 7-A's," I explained above the jangle of strings of bands.

"How old are they?" Giles asked.

"I'm not too sure about prairies," I answered, "but since the flight feathers are just beginning to open up, I'd say about twenty days. We're later than I thought, so I guess we'll have to band about fifty prairies next week."

"Fifty!"

"Yes, give or take ten, depending on how well they do this year," I said.

Before lowering the little falcons back to Jack, I took a picture of Giles—a colorful souvenir of a job well done. In the picture, he is sitting, intoxicated with the five birds, his T-shirt matching their snow-white down; his big black boots are braced against a lichen-covered rock splashed with greens, oranges, and reds; the blue climbing rope is around his waist; and a bright red tackle box filled with silver bands is by his left leg. Although Jack and I had met Giles only twice before, he had soon become one of us—an active part of the research team.

Giles braced himself at my signal, the rope became taut, and then it slackened. Two sharp tugs on the limp line and a loud, drawn-out "OKAY" meant that Jack was free of the rope and standing on firm ground. Shortly, Giles and I were on our way down the rock chimney, no more than fifteen minutes after we had come up.

"How'd that grab you, Giles?" Jack asked as we walked to the truck.

"I must tell you both," Giles said pleasantly, "that was a solid experience—mentally and physically—that I shall long remember. The only wild prairies I have ever seen were in Disney movies. You have no idea how lucky you are to have birds like that. In England, I can drive all day just to see a few ruddy kestrels. This kind of thing has long passed over there. And Indiana wasn't much better."

"That's hard to imagine after being out here now for two summers," I replied.

"Butch, if I were you, I would use that degree you've got in a pitched battle to keep this whole grassland just as it is right now," Giles said.

"Why not like it was a hundred years ago?" Jack added.

"Well, we'll never see that," I lamented, "and that degree you speak of, Giles—any Ph.D. is a flash in the pan when it comes up against the almighty dollar, either trying to limit suburbanization or cultivation, or just getting money to help integrate the advance of man with the activities of birds."

"I guess that is one area of the situation in England that I can look at with some optimism," Giles said. "When the case against DDT was made—and it was an open-and-shut case in England, in the opinion of a lot of people—the damned stuff was banned. Now peregrines are making a comeback. But it was a close call, believe me!"

"How about some breakfast, guys?" I asked as we arrived at the truck.

"What—soda pop and bologna sandwiches?" Jack asked, knowing

the answer. "That's what we've had every meal out here every day for two months, Giles. I've lost a lot of weight."

"Give me a can of soda," Giles said. "I don't think I can stand ground pig stomachs and cow tongues so early in the morning."

"You guys are going to get bloody hungry before evening," I said, trying to imitate Giles's accent while fixing myself a triple-decker sandwich.

Just before we drove off, the female falcon lit on the cliff within ten yards of her eyrie; I had the feeling, as I often did, that her confidence was actually reinforced by her pugnacious attempts to drive us away. We always did go away, and her young were always unharmed.

14

"EVER STOP
FOR TEA?"

"There she blows—the great golden-feathered buzzard of the plains!"
I shouted several minutes after leaving the Breaks Falcon Eyrie.

I was ridiculing my favorite grassland bird: the female eagle at the
Foundation Eyrie. Giles sat up suddenly and straightened his legs to
push himself high onto the back of the seat, so he could thrust his whole
torso out the window.

"Where's an eagle?" he yelled, not knowing in which direction to
look.

"Too late now," I said. "She's gone—disappeared over the cliff top."

We all worked up a sweat walking to the eyrie. Following the
May 21st windstorm, the weather had cleared and warmed again; the
temperature had exceeded eighty-five degrees for the first time that
year on June 1st. But the sunshine was still unwelcome; the inch of May
rain we had had was not ample, even for the arid shortgrass prairie.
The land was cooked much too early in the season. Our sinuses, dry as
dust to the back of our throats, reminded us of the low humidity.

Jack was to band the nearly five-week-old eaglets in their nest;
neither the five-pound male nor the seven-pound female would fit into
the camera bag. Besides, young golden eagles can be feisty at that age;
Jack could expect either cowering or attacking. When a bird is cowering,

169

it usually stands at the far edge of its nest, its back to the intruder and its wings spread but drooping onto the nest surface; the head and neck are held below shoulder level; and the rump is raised slightly, as if the bird is leaning forward. This stance, called "mantling" by falconers, is seen in both wild and captive raptors, particularly as a defensive stand or to conceal food from siblings or a trainer.

The attacking posture is very different, both physically and behaviorally, as Giles had found out at the tree nest earlier in the day. Reaching in to band an eagle on the offense is something to temper one's advances when one is standing precariously on a ledge, hanging from a rope, or clinging to a shaky tree limb. The "ledge act" was Jack's assignment at the Foundation Eyrie.

"Ouch! Dammit!" I heard from my rope-holding position several yards back from the edge of the cliff.

Giles, sitting near the blind snapping pictures, indicated that Jack had just been bitten on the hand. One of the eaglets cowered; the other attacked.

The best way to subdue a hostile eaglet is to place one hand on its back very quickly and then slide the other hand over both feet to pin them to the nest. This leaves the bander one hand short; the alert bird will then bend down and deftly slice a small piece out of the back of the bander's hand with its beak. The bird must be lifted quickly but gently—always by both feet—and cradled safely in the arms or it may strike again. Once restrained, most young raptors, like many wild birds, are quite docile. Those that fight from beginning to end, in defiance of being stroked and addressed in a soft-spoken voice, are exceptions, though it is wise to keep one's chin away from their beaks.

Thus, with only a small hand injury, Jack banded the birds at the Foundation Eyrie: 509–53821 and 509–53822.

As we drove east toward the Indian Eyrie, I recounted a visit to the Foundation Eyrie blind the year before, when the eaglets were about four weeks old. The mother was still feeding them, though they made ineffectual attempts to stand on prey and tear meat from it. At feeding time there was very little competition, as each sat quite erect—back on its haunches, resting on its legs, its feet limply closed out front—awaiting the good favor of its provider.

The most comical nestling behavior at four weeks is the procedure for muting over the nest edge. The digestion of nothing but meat and a little bone produces a dysenteric mixture that would quickly make a

FEMALE GOLDEN EAGLE AND HER YOUNG

sewer of a nest. Each time, they raise their little tails high into the air and wobble backward to the nest edge. With enormous effort to stand high but to lean forward without toppling beak first into the nest, a great catharsis—seemingly with all the beneficial effects of purging, release from tensions, and spiritual renewal—is squirted in a wide arc over the cliff, where it is caught by the wind and drifted onto the rocks and bushes below. But cavity nesters do not always back up toward the open side of the nest; the inside wall is also whitewashed, to a level a few inches higher than the bird can stand.

Also from four weeks of age, and throughout the remaining six weeks of nest life, eaglets develop a nearly insatiable curiosity. As their visual abilities improve, they begin standing high and craning to see things immediately below them, perhaps wood rats carrying off refuse below the eyrie early in the morning; they bob their heads to peer rapidly at some distant object, such as a ground squirrel scurrying near the trail; and they frequently turn their heads upside down to see things above them more clearly.

Birds of prey hunt from above. In their eyes, the upper surfaces of their retinas, which normally perceive the ground, have more sensory cells than the lower surfaces. Thus, if an eagle is on the ground, it often cocks its head sharply to watch a bird overhead with the highly sensitive part of one eye. From the blind, I often detected the presence of an adult by watching for this behavior in nestlings.

"There's what happens if you leave a runt eagle in a nest," I said to Giles as he walked out on the wide ledge at the Indian Eyrie and looked at Abel.

"Doesn't look good to me," he said.

"He looked worse than Tail End Charlie did three weeks ago," Jack said from the cliff top. "Old Witch, over there, beat the hell out of him at first."

Old Witch had done well in her dominance over Abel. At six weeks of age, she was mostly feathered on the upper surface of her wings and between her shoulders; coal-black plumes, in the process of opening, stuck above snow-white down in slightly disordered rows. Abel looked barely four weeks old.

"How about you banding these, Giles?" Jack said to our unsuspecting visitor.

"Not on your life—no way!" Giles exclaimed as he idly tossed a small piece of shredded yucca root in front of Old Witch and got the full-blown lurching attack from her.

She had browbeaten Giles just as she had Abel. I could have given Giles the benefit of the doubt and conceded that he was more intimidated by the forty-five-foot drop-off—but what a great source of sarcastic digs his refusal would make! Had he told us of his phobia, I might not have been so cruel.

"Come on, chicken," I urged, just to make sure. "Jack can easily swing you across to the nest from where he is. It's just a short jump."

"That's quite all right, gentlemen." He declined again, retreating along the ledge toward the security of the cliff top.

He sealed his fate right there; I chided him about it for the rest of the week.

Old Witch and Abel were soon wed to science, each with a ring around one leg; minutes later, the three of us walked past the large boulder, the tiercel's perch, on the way to the truck.

Who banded the birds? Jack, of course; I was not about to step into a nest with such a wicked lady over the edge of a forty-five-foot drop-off. Jack is so much better at climbing; and I do hold a rope well.

"Mayonnaise on your bologna sandwich, Giles?" I said, having finally lured a customer to my prairie menu.

"Oh, my God, no!" he answered, sounding nauseated, "but I sure could use a beer."

"We're miles from the nearest beer," Jack lamented as he snapped open another precious can of pop and started the truck.

"Don't you guys ever stop for tea?" Giles asked several minutes later over his hastily prepared lunch.

"We never stop, Giles—we drop," Jack replied, with a soda-pop belch. "If you think you feel tired now, wait until tonight."

Giles had no idea that we were just warming up to the day's task. One more eagle eyrie—the Cottonwood Eyrie—and the day's "work" would get started. By June 3rd, ours was an endless succession of going to one raptor nest after another to check the number of young and their condition; we always sifted through the nest contents for prey items and noted them in the field book; we banded the birds if they were ready, or determined when we should come back; we observed adult and nestling behavior; we noted dates, wherever possible, of spring arrival, courtship, nest building, copulation, hatching, and fledging; and we looked closely for egg failures and nestling mortalities, and tried to show cause for each death. It was go, go, go, all day long, something that Giles was not totally prepared for.

He was still alert, however, when we neared Raven Tree the second time after banding the bird in the Cottonwood Eyrie.

"Hey, we've got to get Tail End Charlie out of there!" he exclaimed.

"Sure, Giles," I blandly agreed, winking and nodding to Jack. Jack got the message.

"Okay, Giles, but I don't know what you'll do with it," Jack stated as he abandoned the dirt road for the trail to the Chinese elm tree.

"Isn't there another nest we could put it in?" Giles asked.

"Yeah, plenty of them," I said matter-of-factly, "but we can't be messing up the productivity data by shuffling eyases around. Besides, most of the other ferrugs are a week or so ahead of Charlie."

"Don't you have any ferruginous hawks off of the study area?" he asked.

"Not a one," Jack hedged. "We barely have time to cover the study area itself."

"You could always take it home to my wife," I suggested facetiously. "She's a soft touch for taking care of sick hawks, ha-ha!"

"Go on, fetch your blunder," Jack told him as we stopped.

By then, Giles was convinced that he was treading on our toes; yet his compassion would not let him leave the bird there. As he got the hawk, Jack and I quickly decided to put it in a nest we called Sand Creek Ditch, about the only one we knew of in which there were younger ferruginous hawks. But we let Giles stew for a while, unaware of our plan; Charlie's foster home was over fifty miles away, back toward town.

By the time we had visited ten more nests and glassed fifteen Swainson's hawk nests for incubating birds, Giles was noticeably bedraggled by the heat, the altitude, and the excitement. So were Jack and I, although we were used to the necessary hustle and bustle of surveying raptor populations our style.

Once, I glanced at Jack to point out Giles's head-bowed, eyes-closed, but half-smiling posture of dogged satisfaction. His had been an honest labor, as shown by sunburn, fatigue, a few scratches, and a glow from within.

On his lap was an equally disheveled hawk, sleeping half under the edge of its nest—the Englishman's shirt. Giles had fed Charlie to capacity with a dead fledgling meadowlark stolen from another nest we had visited. Quite a predator, that Giles; he tore the prey to pieces as if he had done it before. Charlie made it easy for him, though; seven days old and half starved, the bird was accepting anything red that moved—and many objects of other colors and consistencies. Poor devil! Even I began to feel sorry for the bird.

About six-thirty that evening, Jack went straight ahead at the top of a T in the road, hitting a bumpy trail at fifty miles an hour. Giles, eyes closed again, jumped at the sound of two-dozen pop cans clanking in the bed of a truck, and dumped poor Charlie onto his back, although not onto the floor.

"This is the end of the line for Charlie," I said to Giles, who had a self-satisfied—if sleepy—smile on his face.

"I knew you guys couldn't be as callous as you sounded," he said. "But I must tell you, I cannot detect when you two are pulling my leg."

Giles's mission for the day accomplished, we drove on home. He fell asleep for good on the living-room floor by eight-thirty, exhausted but full of a good dinner and three or four beers; and he was not easy to rouse at five-thirty the next morning! There were too many falcons dancing in his dreams.

Three inches of rain drenched the western edge of our study area on June 6th. Upon returning from the eastern part late that evening, Giles, Jack, and I were surprised to see streams running rampant and making lakes where I had never seen water before. The first major rainstorm of the season (and virtually the last!) apparently had carried clouds with vastly different amounts of water; we had encountered only scattered showers during our meanderings, though we had dodged several thunderstorms—a technique that Giles found quite novel.

We learned more about the main storm's intensity as we journeyed to Battle Gap the next day.

"Look at that bloody fence post," Giles said as he waved at a ranch hand digging a new posthole beside a muddy dirt road.

We all craned our necks to see as Jack motored on about two hundred feet before he realized what had happened.

"Hey, that post was hit by lightning!" Jack exclaimed, slamming on the brakes.

We skidded to a sidewise stop and churned mud in reverse back to the ranch hand.

"Howdy! Looks like the weather made a little work for you," Jack said.

We had met the old guy many times before; he did little else but patrol and repair fences for the local grazing association.

"Yeah, the lightning really blew 'er up," he said, wiping a drop of tobacco juice from his lower lip.

The strike had scattered most of the post about the ground—as far as thirty feet in several directions. The remaining splinters stood like a huge yucca plant with only half a dozen spears. Two of the three wires still hung between the spears, but several feet of the top strand had been cut into two- and three-inch segments by the heat.

Such an awesome force does queer damage. Not five miles away, we found an adult and two young Swainson's hawks lying dead at the base of their nest tree, not a feather out of place: no bullet holes or smashed heads or broken necks. It was a puzzle until Giles noted that most of the bark near the base of the tree was loose and that a large crack coursed several feet upward to where strips of bark had been exploded away. The shock of lightning killed the birds instantly and threw them out of their nest, yet not a single plume was burned.

Later, we checked Raven Tree; everything was fine. At Cattle Pond there had not been much rain, but the wind had dealt the Swainson's hawks another blow—their second nest lay on the ground. They did not nest a third time, but stayed on territory most of the summer.

When we glassed the Indian Eyrie in passing, both birds were still there. Soon we were looking at the ferruginous hawk nest at Battle Gap; no adults were evident, though we could see two large eyases sitting high in their nest.

"They are sure a lot farther along than the ones at Raven Tree," Giles said, glancing through the scope before we got ready for a banding trip to the falcon eyrie around the bluff.

"Maybe we'll be able to band the ferrugs on the way," I said. "It's easier to climb the cliff there, anyway."

The female hawk came to scold us as we climbed. For the most part, though, she stayed out over the gap, having learned that flying and screaming directly over her nest brought one or both prairie falcons down on her. That may have been the reason she had only two young; less troubled cliff- and ground-nesting ferruginous hawks usually have three or four.

We quickly banded the hawks after sending Giles out to the nest first to get some pictures and a closer look at a diving adult ferruginous hawk. She did not disappoint him; the older their young, the more aggressive adult ferruginous hawks become at their nests. Although size somewhat limits their flying skills, heavy female ferrugs swoop swiftly and forcefully.

I visited the Battle Gap ferruginous hawk nest only once more that year—about ten days later—when the eyases were about thirty-five days old, as healthy as could be, and about ten days older than the birds in Raven Tree. What a difference ten days make!

At twenty-five days, the young at Raven Tree had just three rows of feathers showing on their backs, all rows of major feathers. First there was a large sharp **V** of dark feathers—the scapulars—from each shoulder to a point midway down the spine; second was a low-slung **W** of black plumes—the flight feathers—across the lower back and forward along each side; finally, the large tail feathers stuck out two or three inches, with about an inch free of the pinfeather sheaths. The rest of their bodies were covered with snow-white down.

As brooding decreases, it is probably important that the white down of eyases is effectively crisscrossed with black. This destroys the outline and helps conceal them. Raptors are not actually prone to eating each other, but neither do they abstain. Jack has found nestling ferruginous hawks as prey of golden eagles; even predatory birds have predators, and reasons to conceal themselves.

At thirty-five days of age, on the other hand, the young ferruginous hawks at Battle Gap seemed ready to fledge, although feathers still need-ed maturing and muscles needed toning by wing-flapping exercises for another week to ten days.

"Looks like I had better hold the rope this time," I said, looking down the thirty-degree slope toward the cliff edge during our June 7th visit to the Battle Gap prairie falcon eyrie.

By then—about noon—the three of us were all feeling the heat. Giles shed his overshirt and wrapped it around his head, turban style. Jack's face, particularly around his nose, was in perpetual peel. He was the only person I ever knew who never tanned; he just burned all sum-mer. The immediate effects of our labors were also noticeable: quickened respirations, squinting eyes, drying mouths, and foreheads dripping with sweat.

"I'll hold the rope from behind that small rock there at the top of the slope, and we'll double the rope back and down to where you are, Giles," I said as he positioned himself about eight feet back from the edge of the cliff.

There was no reason for having Giles hold the rope; if anything went wrong, Jack and I would both be lying at the bottom of the cliff before Giles felt the slightest tug. Yet, because of the slope down and over the cliff, and the uncomfortable fact that three feet behind me was a twenty-foot drop to a talus slope facing the creek, I felt more secure with Giles also on the line. We had not realized that the cliff top was only thirty feet wide at that point and that it dropped off on both sides.

"Damn, I didn't remember that this eyrie was so overhung," Jack said, looking the situation over from twenty feet to one side. "I'll rappel down once, and if I can't get in, Giles, you'll have to walk down and swing me in with the rope as I go down again."

"Don't hang there too long; I'm not so sure of the spot I'm in," I warned.

With that, Jack heaved the rope overboard, and the female falcon began her counterattack on the plans she had heard from her eyrie. Later, we decided that she might not have heard us; that dark hole we had seen from below, back in April, was about five feet deep.

"Hey, Giles!" Jack yelled from six feet below the edge. "You'd better send me the camera bag. We have to take these birds home."

I could not hear Jack from my spot, so Giles relayed each message.

"He says we have to take them."

"We *what*?" I exclaimed.

It was a cardinal sin to remove a bird from the study area for any reason—or so I thought, because we had never run across this situation before.

"He says they're sick," Giles said as he crawled nearer to the edge of the cliff carrying his end of the rope.

"How sick?" I asked.

By that time, Jack had started swinging on the rope to get into the eyrie by himself. That changed my thoughts to more immediate concerns.

"Tell him to hurry up or he's going to be in for a long fall," I told Giles. "I can't hold out much longer."

Giles transmitted my message, but all he got back were some words muffled by six feet of rock; Jack was headfirst to his waist in the hole trying to get the young birds, which were just out of reach. For some reason, the rope never slackened and I kept pulling on Jack's lifeline, growing more fatigued all the while. Actually, I was working against him. He was grunting, straining, cussing, and trying to get enough slack in the rope to reach the birds, while I was collecting every inch of slack and more.

About then, Giles looked down at his feet and discovered flickering daylight through a two-inch crack in the whole bluff. It was Jack's T-shirt directly below him.

"Hey, this damn cliff is split all along here," Giles said excitedly.

"Oh, neat! Just tell him to hurry up!"

The situation was so serious it was funny. Misinterpretation of a climber's needs and position can be fatal. Here was a helpless Englishman standing on a fault in the cliff, not knowing if the crack was old or new; he held a section of rope that meant nothing to the problem at hand; and he wanted to help, but his fear of heights kept him several feet back from the edge. Meanwhile, Jack was suffering from exhaustion and near heatstroke trying to get into the eyrie while I kept pulling him out of it. The only useful thing Giles did was to talk strength into a failing rope holder, who could have remedied the difficult situation just by giving the climber a little slack.

But our path of communication was muffled; our only references were our own. Giles had six holes in his dike and only five free fingers.

Somehow Jack finally accomplished his herculean task.

"Hey, guys, I almost died up there," he said, several minutes later, when we met him at the bottom of the cliff.

"I just could not hear you there for a while," Giles said.

"That's got to be the worst," Jack continued. "After I got the birds, I'd look up at the cliff and see it silhouetted against the sky. Everything would kinda go real dark, and then it would come back and get light again. And I was screaming at the top of my lungs. But all I could get out of you was a distant 'What?'"

"I was really concerned," Giles said, "but I could not for the life of me understand you."

"Butch, you almost pulled me off the cliff," Jack said.

"Hell, I just did the only thing I knew to do, and that was to pull," I answered.

"That eyrie is terrible," Jack went on, "but those prairies were getting eaten alive, and I had to get them out of there."

"What do you mean eaten alive?" I asked.

"Go take a look at them—and there's a dead one about ten feet from the bag," Jack said. "It's been dead for several days."

Each of the birds was seriously infected with hundreds of blood-sucking tick larvae, particularly around the eyes. The parasites had gorged themselves with blood, literally draining life from their host falcons in the process. Giles had a few more afflicted birds to worry over, but there was little he could do. The whole shabby matter was a downer. On the way home and to the veterinarian, we discovered that the birds were all blind or nearly so. None recovered. Our list of natural causes of nest failure was growing; in subsequent days we found two more broods of prairie falcons infested with ticks, one of which was wiped out completely.

Giles spent two days getting a line on a job and renting a house. With a stroke of luck, he accomplished both and then promptly departed to Indiana to bring his wife and all their worldly belongings out West. He was determined to do his own thing, at least part of the time, even though he sensed that his next visit to the prairie would not be as vivid as his first week there.

He had experienced the full gamut of emotions involved in studying raptors: the solitude of visiting remote places, the anxieties of climbing, the surprise of unexpected face-to-face encounters with aggressive nestlings, the thrill of learning new facts about ecology, the camaraderie of friends with similar motivations, the satisfaction of helping troubled animals, and the torment of dead or dying raptors—electrocuted by lightning, blown to the ground by wind, or eaten alive and blinded by parasites. To use his own words, his first week on the shortgrass prairie was the most exciting and most instantly rewarding outdoor experience he had ever had.

"See you about a month hence," he said when he left.

15

FLEDGING:
A HOLLOW
PROMISE

Fledging conveys independence to a bird—safety from the uncertain shelter of its nest. Because downy raptors sharpen the excitement of my living, my emotions are mixed about seeing the birds I have worked with fly away. But my empathy, wishing them flight, prevails; the failures of ground school, addled eggs and dead eyases, are even more repulsive—putrid, drabbled, and without potential for new life in the next generation—than the usual obituaries gained through band returns.

Unfortunately, even the great promise of an eyrie full of healthy fledgling falcons or eagles is itself somewhat hollow. According to nature's rules, at least three out of every four or five fledgling raptors never reach the age of one year. Therein lies the source of mixed emotions. This high juvenile mortality is due primarily to starvation and other natural misfortunes. Hunter's rifles, predator-control poisons, automobiles, and power lines that electrocute raptors—all taken together—are not nearly as destructive of young raptors as nature itself.

One critical part of the post-fledging period for a bird is the week following its first flight. The problem was well illustrated when Jack and I visited the Breaks Falcon Eyrie to count fledglings on June 23rd. Usually, young prairie falcons spend several days hopping and flapping

PRAIRIE FALCONS READY TO FLEDGE

from ledge to ledge near their eyries, but that was not the way of one young tiercel, the most adventurous of the five at the eyrie.

"There's a falcon just ahead of us," Jack said, pointing to the bird sitting on sod barely fifty feet from the trail—but three hundred yards from its eyrie!

"We'd better get it back to the cliff," I said. "I could do without an early band return on it."

There were many dangers in the young tiercel's walking exploits: coyotes can readily run down poorly flighted birds; golden eagles sometimes kill easily caught prairie falcons and feed them to their eaglets; and inquisitive cattle will surround a grounded raptor and then stampede if a curious steer jumps suddenly when it is grabbed on the nose by defensive talons.

Jack caught the callow wanderer easily after it lay down to hide from his advance. The little fellow became aggressive just before being picked up but did not attempt to fly.

While Jack carried the bird back to the cliff and placed him on the safety of a low ledge near the eyrie, I observed the young falcons in the nest. There were just three; the other was on a ledge several yards away. All were extremely curious about that unfeathered two-legged thing walking toward them and carrying one of their nestmates.

Jack was nearly back to the truck before their mother—their provider!—flew in. Heedless of her alarm calls, all five youngsters screamed incessantly, more hungry than fearful of what they had just experienced, more inclined to join their parent in the freedom of flight than to remain in their dusty eyrie another day.

Jack and I logged visits to eight prairie falcon eyries on June 23rd: the Breaks Falcon Eyrie, Capped Rock, Twin Gates, Beehive, and others. We were working extra hours in order to count all fledgling prairie falcons, golden eagles, and ferruginous hawks before Jack had to leave the study to make a living doing someone else's thing—at least temporarily. Not only the season, but also the money was running out. It was hard to believe that almost three months had passed since the day Jack confidently announced, "Look, dammit—you think and I'll drive! And we'll show them how many hawks there really are around here."

We had found more eyries than I thought possible; my hypothesis that two men could do three to five times as much field work as one man had been proved to my satisfaction. In some ways, we even exceeded our capabilities; many of the young prairie falcons never were banded. There were over fifty, as I had told Giles. In addition, some eyries were so overhung by rock that special time-consuming climbing techniques would have been necessary. In such instances—and at Beehive, where workers came and went only a few feet from the eyases—Jack merely counted the fledglings as he rappelled past.

In all, three of twenty-seven nestings of prairie falcons failed completely during the two years of intensive study: two because of tick larvae and another owing, apparently, to bobcat predation. Such fruitless attempts entered the field notebook as important—but cheerless—zeros. That downward tug on productivity brought the average number of prairie falcons fledged per eyrie down to about three and a half—still the highest ever recorded for the species, to my knowledge, and three times as many as during another study in the same general area during the early 1960s.

Our count of fledgling eaglets was lower than that of prairie falcons, though an average of just over one eaglet per nesting attempt was comparable to other studies in different areas through the years.

On Jack's last day afield, June 30th, our work took us past the Indian Eyrie—Abel and Old Witch, the only remaining uncertainties in our final count of eaglets. We climbed the Breaks along a route west of the eyrie, from which we could see the birds without unduly alarming them. It was no time to go into the nest, because Old Witch was old enough to fledge prematurely and, possibly, to break a leg or a wing at the end of a futile first flight.

Presumably, both birds watched us closely, though we could not see Abel until we were halfway up. Old Witch's physical bloom made Abel look positively wilted. Her broad shoulders and perfect plumage embodied most of the fine qualities of her mother: beauty, strength, superiority, promise. She had less than a week left in the nest.

"Maybe her leaving will be Abel's salvation," I told Jack hopefully.

"Boy, I don't know," he said. "It'll be ten days or more before he finishes feathering on the head."

"Yeah, but if he doesn't have to compete with her, he'll do better," I said.

"But will the adults keep feeding him?" Jack asked.

Some believe that if an eaglet is slow to leave its nest, the parents deliberately starve it into fledging—a seemingly dead-end street for an inferior nestling. There is no doubt that adults bring—and eyases eat—less food when fledging is imminent. This preflight fasting may be just a natural trimming down from a fat nestling with blood-filled quills and bones to a muscular fledgling with many hollow bones and soon-to-be dry feathers—a finished product capable of flight. It is possible that parent raptors "know," instinctively, the lower food requirements of their young during the final weeks of nest life; the pace of food gathering decreases accordingly.

We left the Indian Eyrie still uncertain of Abel's fate.

Food was not being held back from the eyases at the Antelope Reservoir Swainson's hawk nest, our next stop. While we made fledgling counts of other species, we also pushed hard to find those Swainson's hawk nests that we had not found earlier. With Jack leaving, the banding and counting of fledgling Swainson's hawks during late July and early August was to be my responsibility.

Birds other than the common species we had known during spring greeted us that hot afternoon. Water birds, such as California gulls, black terns, and American coots, were as evident as mallards, redheads, and avocets. Land birds—brown thrashers, kingbirds, shrikes, Bullock's orioles, grackles, blackbirds, and several kinds of sparrows—helped the more abundant species alert the hawks to our advance. We also found the two young owls and one adult perched near our usual parking place, but they were not disturbed even though the hawks still harassed them at every opportunity.

It was to be a long-standing battle; families of horned owls usually stay together near their nest groves for months—sometimes into November! Actually, the owls had nowhere else to go until other raptors finished nesting and moved about more widely. In the meantime, their least vulnerable perches were in trees along the west bank of the reservoir, far away from its north end where the hawk nest had survived all the storms. That bundle of tumbleweeds and twigs, although not very substantial in itself, was well placed in a three-armed crotch barely five feet from the main trunk.

The three young Swainson's hawks were a week old on June 30th. Each had a full crop, and two freshly killed lark buntings lay alongside a decapitated meadowlark on the nest rim. All the prey were fledglings.

Most Swainson's hawks hatch as lark buntings begin to fledge—during the last two weeks of June. Young buntings stay in their nests for only eight or nine days, and then spend a week or more flopping across the prairie unable to fly more than a few yards. About eight out of every ten prey fed to eyas Swainson's hawks in late June are fledgling birds, half of them lark buntings. I once thought it coincidence that the migratory and numerically dominant buteo depends so heavily on fledglings

of a migratory and numerically dominant passerine bird as food. And more, it could be chance that their breeding cycles are just enough out of phase for the parent hawks to provide newly hatched eyases with easily caught fledgling lark buntings.

But a similar hatching-time and fledging-time relationship exists near the Breaks between ferruginous hawks and the first broods of horned larks. Although birds account for only four of every ten prey fed to hatchling ferruginous hawks in late May, two of the four birds are fledgling horned larks. The relatively sedentary and second most common buteo frequently preys on the also relatively sedentary and second most abundant passerine bird.

Yet ferruginous hawks kill fledgling lark buntings only rarely in late June and early July. Their use of fledgling passerines is short-lived. As eyas hawks grow, it becomes inefficient to feed them small birds; adults, more and more, bring larger prey—thirteen-lined ground squirrels, cottontails, jackrabbits, and meadowlarks—to their ravenous young.

During the first two weeks of July, there are so many young ground squirrels emerging from their underground dens that even the masters of opportunism, Swainson's hawks, switch quickly to eating more mammals: from 20 percent of the diet in late June to 70 percent in early July. Young Swainson's hawks complete their growth during the hottest time of the year on a diet of half mammals and half birds, with a few salamanders and snakes for variety. These relationships and percentages must vary from year to year, though the generalities of predator-prey interactions from week to week within a given season are remarkable.

July and early-August temperatures rarely exceeded one hundred degrees in 1972, but a continual lashing of eighty-five- and ninety-degree direct sunlight began to brown the greening of April and May. Cool-season grasses withered quickly; winter wheat stood golden until it was harvested in mid-July; and the pale, creamy, somewhat bell-shaped blossoms of yucca were too soon reduced to dry seed pods.

When the hottest weather came, the productivity of all prairie falcons, golden eagles, and great horned owls and all but a few pairs of ferruginous hawks was known. With Jack gone, my tasks were to keep tabs on seventy pairs of Swainson's hawks, to follow up on individual birds, and to collect data that were passed up earlier to keep nest visits brief— data such as nest height, diameter, depth, and exposure to the sun. Even a description of the habitat surrounding each nest site was important to me for later estimates of how many more large raptors could inhabit the shortgrass prairie.

By July 8th, Giles had completed his move from Indiana. He spent that day afield with me nearly as frantic as he had been five weeks earlier to see some wild hawks. As I expected, he wanted to check on Tail End Charlie and Abel. Sand Creek Ditch, Charlie's foster nest, was not far from town, so we stopped there first.

"Charlie is forty-five days old today," I said, with the nest tree in sight, "if he isn't dead. They usually fledge in forty-two days."

"He had bloody well better not be dead—else I will hold you personally responsible," Giles said.

"Well, you know how the pendulum of nature swings, Giles," I said, in fun.

"I shall wrap the pendulum of nature around your neck if that bird is not there," he threatened, having learned to dish out a little benign ill humor of his own.

Although the nest at Sand Creek Ditch was visible from a well-traveled road, Jack and I had not taken time to band the birds there. I was confident that Charlie would be waiting for Giles, though, for I had checked on the birds with the scope several times, and the land was posted "No Trespassing." Ferruginous hawks that nested on posted or remote land fledged nearly twice as many young, on the average, as those that nested at sites freely accessible to the public. Other species showed a similar trend.

The real question was whether the parent hawks had accepted an extra nestling. A year earlier, we had placed an eaglet in a foster nest after its mother had been shot, electrocuted, or killed some other way. The foster eaglet had been reared, and it subsequently fledged.

"We didn't get here any too early," Giles said, pointing to a hawk sitting on a fence post near the nest.

"Are you going to chase it down or am I?" I asked.

Looking up at the nest, I added, "You can band the two in the nest, and I'll chase."

To my surprise, he agreed; he had lost his fear of heights somewhere—at least the first fifteen feet of it. He had his charges banded within minutes.

I had a little more difficulty. The fence post made a fine launching pad for the partially flighted hawk, which watched my approach for a time but finally flew unsteadily down a gentle slope. Its wingbeats were exaggerated—deeper than an adult's—as if it were doing the breaststroke. Its landing was a straightforward but brief run, with momentum unbroken by spread wings. Comically, the bird crashed forward onto its head and breast before stopping completely. We concluded that it was Tail End Charlie, because the other two, although feathered, showed no inclination to leave their nest. He had probably fledged the day before.

From his crash site, Charlie led me another quarter-mile before he turned to fight. As usual, I got one hand on his back, the other over his feet, yelled "Ouch, dammit!" when he bit me, and then lifted him into my arms.

Back at the nest, Giles placed the band on while I cradled the bird firmly. Charlie seemed indignant when I placed him on a branch, but he was alive and well—very well, considering his dreary beginning! Giles was convinced that he had saved Charlie's life. Perhaps he had.

As we neared the Breaks an hour later, we checked Raven Tree, Charlie's original nest, where but one fledgling remained. Even before we stopped the truck, the bird flew off much more effectively than Charlie had, but still with deep, half-learned wingbeats. It rose to at least a hundred feet and covered half a mile before disappearing over a small undulation of grassland. Fortunately, it had been banded two weeks earlier; we drove on, reassured that Charlie's brother and two sisters had also fledged.

Next came Abel. I tried not to communicate my concern for the ill-fated fellow to Giles, but he sensed it.

"You're not too sure of yourself on this one, are you?" he asked as we passed the stone Indian shelters.

"No," I answered, with a sigh that was not completely scientific.

It is too easy to get close to an eagle emotionally, especially one that may be a loser.

"Even if he makes it out of the nest," I continued, "he's got an uphill battle to keep from starving to death."

I did not fully appreciate at the time—though I had read it—that families of golden eagles are usually quite close-knit for several months after the young fledge. In fact, parent eagles are more attentive to their flighted young than to nestlings during the ninth and tenth weeks in their eyries. Young golden eagles are fed by their parents into October and November, though the juveniles are pursuing and catching a few things for themselves before then.

One thing is certain: the bonds between golden eagles and their fledged young are stronger than the parent-offspring associations of most

animals, including most other birds and many mammals. Preparation for the next breeding season probably severs the most lasting family ties, though the details of golden eagle post-fledging behavior are largely unknown. Even when subadult eagles are completely independent, they are tolerated casually in the nesting territories of adults. Apparently, this passiveness continues until young birds are in full adult plumage, three and a half years after hatching.

If Abel could just get out of his nest, he would have a chance, with the extended period of parental care, to survive.

When we rounded the jut in the cliff that hid the Indian Eyrie along the usual approach, I immediately spotted an eagle sitting on the tiercel's rock. Because the base of its tail was white, I knew it was one of the young eagles, probably Old Witch. I swung the scope to the pile of sticks—past the heavy whitewash below the narrow ledge where the prairie falcons perched in winter. The nest was capped by a thin dark mass, just as it had been when I found the Indian Eyrie the year before, but I was unable to see movement.

We drove closer, forcing Old Witch to fly off along the cliff. That brought Abel to his feet in fine, full feather to give the typical begging yelp—"weeeo-hyo-hyo-hyo"—in anticipation of food or flight or both. He shut up and lay back down again as Giles and I jubilantly left the truck.

At the eyrie, we found the object of our affections healthy, obnoxious, gorged with rabbit, and lying next to most of another cottontail. Development had taken Abel seventy-three days, a week or so longer than most golden eagles. We knew he would fledge, at least.

As far as nesting golden eagles were concerned, the study ended where it had begun each summer: a short distance from a broken foundation and a stone-lined ice cellar of an abandoned farmstead. Being so close to the Foundation Eyrie, I could not resist taking Giles by once more. It was a nostalgic experience.

"You know, Giles," I said, "I never dreamed years ago that I would know a family of eagles as intimately as I do the ones at the Foundation Eyrie. It's going to be hard to leave this place."

"I can imagine," he said, shaking his head sadly.

"I guess the most personally gratifying thing I've gained out here," I said, "is confidence in the environment—at least in the shortgrass prairie. Seeing these birds doing so well year after year at a time when many other people think that all raptors are doing poorly was a great lesson to learn firsthand."

Giles opened and closed the gate below the Foundation Eyrie; then we drove a hundred feet farther and parked where we could look into the nest from a distance but almost on a level with it. We left three and a half hours later, having been captivated the whole time by two fully feathered eaglets, sixty-eight and sixty-nine days old, about to make their first flight.

"I suppose there'll have to be a change of the general public's attitude," I said, "to keep some populations of birds of prey from declining further, but the question in my mind now is not *if* there will be raptors for my kids to enjoy, but how many. That's the opposite of what I was wondering a year and a half ago."

"I must admit that I sleep better at night having seen this place," Giles said.

Of course our optimism that day—and now—does not apply everywhere. But it makes little difference if one gazes down the Columbia River in Washington State, or on the great walls of the Snake River Canyon in Idaho, or on the many desert cliffs and grasslands of the Great Basin, or on the prairie just east of the Rocky Mountains; places like the Eagle Breaks—where natural selective processes still designate those animals which will carry new life toward future generations—can dispel the fears some have about our environment. Admittedly, proper care and management of animal populations and habitats will be needed. But there is room for more confidence in Mother Earth than some now have.

As Giles and I talked, the Foundation Eyrie eaglets spent much of their time wing flapping, a behavior that had been increasing in frequency and intensity for five weeks. Usually they gripped the yucca spears and sticks to keep from rising, though often they actually hovered rather awkwardly several inches above the nest, gingerly touching down with one foot or the other every few seconds. Of course, only one bird could flap at a time. Giles and I almost suffocated with laughter when both tried; first one began, and the other knocked it down by joining in. The next time, the roles were reversed, but the result was always the same: a pile of disoriented eagle feathers lying flat on the nest.

Fortunately, we were able to leave in a jovial mood. I will never forget the last I saw of those eagles in their eyrie: they were both looking at something directly below the nest, perhaps a lizard or a young cliff swallow perched on a rock of the broken foundation. The freedom of flight would soon be theirs, and all too soon I would be on my way to a much different land—the Pacific Northwest—to live.

My years on the prairie had been a long, often strenuous, often dangerous experience—an uncomfortable adventure at times. But I was suntanned, in good physical condition, and possessed by a much more satisfied outlook on life than I had had before coming to know the Eagle Breaks. Some of the birds did not fare nearly as well at the hands of nature; nor did the equipment. The truck, brand-new at the beginning of the season, was a shambles. The spotting scope needed adjustment; the camera was dirty, inside and out; and the tape recorder had quit several weeks before. I came away with several files full of data cards, a few notebooks, several hundred photographs, and a head spinning with ideas and stories to develop and to tell. There remained only the memories, and the excitement of discovering new facts and relationships in the data.

YOUNG EAGLES READY TO FLEDGE

EPILOGUE

Indians vacated the rock shelters near the Indian Eyrie during the mid- to late 1800s—as white men came. Golden eagles then moved back into that territory. The parents of the rancher who told me about the Foundation Eyrie were forced from the house below the eyrie by the drought of the 1930s; another eagle territory became available. The areas near these nesting places, as well as those near Honey Locust Shack, Raven Tree, and countless other man-created situations, have been unpeopled only since the dust-bowl days.

Today birds of prey are abundant near the Eagle Breaks and in similar habitats throughout the western United States as a result, in large part, of people moving from once inhabited arid land to irrigable fields or to cities and towns. Wildlife has been permitted to reoccupy the scarred but reclaimable habitat. Now the direction of nature is set by ecological succession back toward original conditions and by current land-use practices—both of which allow raptors to nest in many places where they could not have nested during the early decades of white settlement or, in many instances, before the coming of white men.

But the indirect improvements of habitat and subsequent re-establishment of wildlife—particularly after an abuse by man—are often overlooked in man's evaluation of his detrimental effects on creatures and beasts of the field. We should, however, evaluate the beneficial effects of the mismanagement of nature, too, even though the bright side may be small compared to the losses. There are lessons to be learned from these losses.

For example, nearly a third of all large raptors nesting within fifty miles of the Eagle Breaks do so in man-created situations. Primarily, this involves hawks, eagles, and owls nesting in trees transplanted to previously treeless prairie by early farmers and cattlemen. Though many of these trees are now past prime, they still stand near abandoned farmsteads and ditches, man-made ponds, and both operating and nonoperating windmills.

Only prairie falcons, whose nesting cliffs stand virtually unaltered by man, have not benefited directly from the early farmers who taught us a valuable lesson about birds of prey by failing to domesticate the prairie soils. Inadvertently, it was shown—even before we became concerned about the future of raptor populations—that grassland birds of prey can be managed in the wild, an idea complicated by the fact that man has been both the destroyer and the mender.

Management will not be as simple for all the world's birds of prey as merely planting trees. Nevertheless, the response of grassland buteos, in particular, hints that other raptors may adapt readily to purposeful management—when and where necessary—such as digging nesting cavities for prairie falcons in unsatisfactory cliffs or providing artificial nest structures on sandy creek banks and in monotonous expanses of grasslands for eagles.

A parallel situation, where inadvertent benefits to wildlife are ignored, involves today's ranchers. In general, the attitudes toward birds of prey of the ranchers I encountered pleased me. Admittedly, nearly all were cattlemen, but I still do not believe the doomsday prophecy that golden eagles—or any other raptors—will be poisoned and shot into extinction by sheepmen. Nor do I condone the ecological and sometimes illegal shortcomings of sheep ranching. It must be understood, however, that although the livestock industry may be the nemesis of eagles in some parts of North America, *most* ranchers are benefactors of eagles. Grazing land is a place for birds of prey to reproduce—at least! Cultivation inhibits—even prevents—breeding in many places. Near the Eagle Breaks, only four out of every hundred pairs of large raptors nested in trees that were surrounded primarily by cultivated land; and nearly all that did were Swainson's hawks.

If radical conservationists need a cause, limiting cultivation—not tormenting ranchers—is it!

Furthermore, ranchers fence their land, post it with "No Trespassing" signs, and frequently patrol it; nothing could benefit nesting birds more. Yet because the ranchers' conservation is not intentional, it is rarely credited in their favor. Instead, protectionists, through the news media, put a rifle in one hand (and poison in the other) of every ranchman in the West each time the abuses of a few lawbreaking sheepmen are discovered. In reality, the facts support neither the errant sheep ranchers nor the uncompromising protectionists.

Another sensitive issue that was placed in better perspective for me by my grassland studies was the false notion that *all* birds of prey were proceeding rapidly toward extinction because of pesticides. When I began my studies near the Eagle Breaks back in March of 1971, there was so much uproar about pesticides that I almost expected to find falcons, eagles, hawks, and owls flopping on the ground in the throes of collapsing nerve and muscular functions, the results of acute poisoning. If not that, at least I was certain to find crushed eggs in most nests, since DDT and other chlorinated hydrocarbons, as the serious offenders are called, affect calcium metabolism and cause birds to lay thin-shelled eggs.

But I found no brainsick birds, crushed eggs, or any other evidence that the birds of prey were doing anything but reproducing normally in the two thousand square miles ultimately chosen as an extensive study area. There were problems from one year to the next, but I searched for and found possible reasons for variations in the numbers and productivities of raptors in the field, not in a chemist's laboratory. The relative unimportance of chemical poisoning was probably due, in part, to the aridity of the shortgrass prairie. Many raptors that prey on water birds and fish *are* seriously affected by chemical pollutants, because the poisons move more readily in aquatic environments; peregrine falcons, bald eagles, ospreys, and brown pelicans are good examples.

Not so with the raptors of the arid shortgrass prairie! I used to feel a great urgency to study raptors before their populations declined so far that even the slightest interference with them would be unwarranted. But no more! In the shortgrass prairie, an alarmist would trip over his own dominoes. Just because the peregrine falcon and a few other species are thought to be declining in numbers, this does not mean that the prairie falcon and golden eagle will also fall, followed by the buteos and all other raptors.

Perhaps mine was a study of raptors in a land of promise. As my research at the Eagle Breaks neared an end, I was not at all apprehensive—and justifiably so—about the future of the raptor populations with which I was working. I had time to fret about little matters, such as individual birds—Abel, Tail End Charlie, and the tick-infested prairie falcons; about specific nest sites where failures might be averted through proper management—the Oil Well Eyrie, Cattle Pond, and many others; and about ways to permit more uniform use of the prairie by raptors. When one gets down to cases, there are places for positive management of raptorial birds all around the Eagle Breaks and elsewhere, but there is no room for despair.

We will get nowhere by sitting back and expecting too much from nature, all the while castigating ourselves by throwing stones at other segments of society. The stones we cast are chipped with guilt. Everyone takes up space; everyone eats; and everyone uses energy. The problem is that it is both easy and fashionable to cast stones; but it is much too difficult for the general public to put the alarmists' notions into proper perspective.

There is far more need for people to pull the raptor-conservation bandwagon than there is need for people to jump on it. Total protection has both biological and political shortcomings. One actually weakens the impact of calling something endangered, for example, if everything is said to be endangered. There is too much possibility of the general reaction "If all birds of prey are going extinct, why try to save any of them? It is already too late."

It is not too late! Nature is still doing many things correctly and on cue, and bird populations, given half a chance, are remarkably resilient. But we must not expect above-normal production from birds, as I once did. Much less than perfection is required, because success rates are just part of a larger scheme—that is, the balance that develops from the rate of successfully rearing young, the death rate of each species, and the number of individuals that can be supported by the available habitat.

Yet these natural relationships must be reinforced by the attitudes of men. There is need for change here—for the creation of a compromise worked out by strict conservationists, ranchers, the users of pesticides, and others who interact positively or negatively with raptors.

And more steps need to be taken beyond a change in attitude. The task ahead must include considerable research on raptor-management techniques followed by conservative application of those methods which are found suitable. No one wishes to see golden eagles, peregrine falcons,

IMMATURE GOLDEN EAGLE

and other birds of prey vanish from the earth because of inadequate knowledge of their biological needs or a lack of information on how to manage them in the wild. Their needs are their message to mankind, as it came to me at the Foundation Eyrie.

The lesson of the Eagle Breaks, then, is not that all birds of prey everywhere are reproducing normally; the lesson is not that there has been a reversal of recent regional declines of some raptor populations. Rather, study of the Eagle Breaks has revealed alternatives for increasing existing raptor populations, slowing declines, and restoring extirpated populations. Every North American species of raptor, except possibly the California condor, occurs in sufficient numbers for active management research—and for actual management!

But man not only poses a potential threat to the success of each raptor nest; he also is responsible for the ultimate survival of raptorial species. The predatory chain leads to *Homo sapiens* in but one more link. Although man's predation on eagles and other birds of prey is usually more subtle and indirect than the eagle's grip on a rabbit, it unfortunately can be equally harsh. But, unlike the eagle, man can be selective and compassionate in his position at the end of the chain. Will he be? He must, of course. To leave birds of prey unattended in man's world may lead them to extinction long before their time.

The alternative is management—*applied* conservation of raptors— if and when it is needed.

A NOTE
ABOUT THE AUTHOR

Richard R. Olendorff was born in Parsons, Kansas,
and now lives in Annandale, Virginia. After a childhood
spent in Alaska and undergraduate study at the University
of Washington, he received a Ph.D. degree in zoology
from Colorado State University. From 1971 to 1975 he was
first a Frank M. Chapman Post-doctoral Fellow and then
a Field Associate of the Department of Ornithology at
The American Museum of Natural History in New York.
Dr. Olendorff is currently a wildlife management biologist
with the Bureau of Land Management of the Department
of the Interior in Washington, D. C.

A NOTE
ABOUT THE ILLUSTRATOR

Robert Katona was born in Athens, Ohio, but has lived
most of his life in Golden, Colorado. A self-taught artist,
he has trained and flown many different hawks and falcons,
and his familiarity with birds of prey has led to illustration
contributions to the Raptor Research Foundation and the
North American Peregrine Foundation. He has won the
Jenkins Award twice at the Gilpin County Arts Association
Show, and his paintings have been exhibited in several
galleries, including the Denver Art Museum and the
Kennedy Galleries in New York.

A NOTE ON THE TYPE

The text of this book was set in film in a typeface called Griffo, a camera version of Bembo, the well-known monotype face. The original cutting of Bembo was made by Francesco Griffo of Bologna only a few years after Columbus discovered America. It was named for Pietro Bembo, the celebrated Renaissance writer and humanist scholar who was made a cardinal and served as secretary to Pope Leo X.

Sturdy, well balanced, and finely proportioned, Bembo is a face of rare beauty. It is, at the same time, extremely legible in all of its sizes.

The book was composed by Superior Printing, Champaign, Illinois; printed and bound by Halliday Lithograph Corporation, West Hanover, Massachusetts.

The book was designed by Earl Tidwell.